MOST UNLIKELY TO SUCCEED
Letters to Those Who Loved Me When I Couldn't Love Myself

Donald Whitehead

Dear Linda

iUniverse

God Bless you
Donald W Whitehead

MOST UNLIKELY TO SUCCEED
LETTERS TO THOSE WHO LOVED ME
WHEN I COULDN'T LOVE MYSELF

Copyright © 2020 Donald Whitehead.

All rights reserved. No part of this book may be used or reproduced by any means, graphic, electronic, or mechanical, including photocopying, recording, taping or by any information storage retrieval system without the written permission of the author except in the case of brief quotations embodied in critical articles and reviews.

iUniverse books may be ordered through booksellers or by contacting:

iUniverse
1663 Liberty Drive
Bloomington, IN 47403
www.iuniverse.com
1-800-Authors (1-800-288-4677)

Because of the dynamic nature of the Internet, any web addresses or links contained in this book may have changed since publication and may no longer be valid. The views expressed in this work are solely those of the author and do not necessarily reflect the views of the publisher, and the publisher hereby disclaims any responsibility for them.

Any people depicted in stock imagery provided by Getty Images are models, and such images are being used for illustrative purposes only. Certain stock imagery © Getty Images.

ISBN: 978-1-5320-9631-0 (sc)
ISBN: 978-1-5320-9646-4 (e)

Print information available on the last page.

iUniverse rev. date: 02/28/2020

Table of Contents

Acknowledgements ix
Chapter 1: At the Beginning…the End 1
Chapter 2: Long Ago and Far Away 8
Chapter 3: Early Family Days 13
Chapter 4: My Father 19
Chapter 5: Academic Highs…and Lows 24
Chapter 6: Academic Losses 32
Chapter 7: College? The Military? Two for the Price of One 39
Chapter 8: I Attack the U.S. Navy 47
Chapter 9: The Navy Returns Fire 55
Chapter 10: My Meet Up with Cocaine 74
Chapter 11: First Steps Out 80
Chapter 12: A Small Success and a Great Tragedy 87
Chapter 13: More Steps Up and…an Emmy? 91
Chapter 14: The National Coalition 98
Chapter 15: Tragedy: No Other Word 105
Chapter 16: A Different Kind of Recovery 111
Chapter 17: Tracy 117
Chapter 18: At the End…the Start 124
Epilogue 133

The book is dedicated to memories of Kadeash, Channing, and Little David. Although you left us far too soon we are grateful to God for allowing us to share your lives with us. You are truly missed.

Acknowledgements

Above all, I thank God, the maker and ruler of all creation, for being who He is. I thank Him for giving life and breath to all; for scripting the days and times; for saving and changing lives through the revelation of Himself and His glory that is Jesus; for unraveling hearts and continuously turning them toward home; and for being all and greater than all. I thank God for creating and unfolding His perfect plan. I thank Him for His forgiveness. I thank Him for forgiving me. God has always been an important part of my life. I pray often and enjoy my personal relationship with Him. One of the most painful parts of my story is the strain on my relationship with God. At times it seemed as if I was ignoring my relationship, believing God wouldn't know how I was living.

Writing *Most Unlikely to Succeed* was a soul stirring experience and a collaborative effort. I bounced ideas and sought feedback from supportive friends and family. Thank you to John Briggs, Michelle Budzek, my sister Carmen Broomfield, my incredible mother Carolyn Whitehead-Brown, and my amazing wife Tracy Quinichett Whitehead for the enormous amount of time invested in editing and sharing personal insights.

My family inspired, cared for, and encouraged me: my sisters and brothers, (Sherri, Carmen, Angie, Darrin, and

David); the Thurmonds; my dad, Donald Hugh Whitehead Sr.(*for giving me life*); my aunts, (Pat, Peggy, Thelma, Theresa, Mary Lou, and Jerri); my uncles, (Marky, Bill, Bobby, and Nelson); my cousins, (Ink, Mary, Tony, Big Ed, Donna, Donita, and Burnetta, Arnold, Greg, Mary, Michelle, Calvin, Diane, Jeanette, Yvonne, Jean, and Nissa); and my nieces and nephews, too many to name individually. A heartfelt thanks to each of you for loving me when I could not love myself.

Many institutions were my shelter from the storm of hopelessness. A sincere thanks to the staff at the Drop Inn Center, especially Bonnie, Ed, Pat, Andy, Amy and buddy; ReStoc; and The Greater Cincinnati Coalition for the Homeless staff and board, Mary Burke, Fannie Johnson, Cliff Jones, Katy Heins, Donna Howard, Jimmy Heath, Susan Knight, Gina, Tammy, and others. I will always remember and be grateful for my friends from the rooms, Glen C., Bill J., Merrick C., Greg P., Denise W., Carla H., Courtney, Diana R.H., Alvin E., Veronica R., Dan H., Monte J., Michael J., Danny L., Dwight H., William B., Kim, Otis, Andy, Jeff R., and Michael.

For countless positive life altering experiences: I thank the staff and Board of the COHHIO; NCH; Ohio Valley Goodwill; Goodwill of Greater Washington; St. Vincent de Paul; Recovery Hotel; The Cincinnati Health Network; The Cincinnati Continuum of Care Inc.; and The Baltimore Healthcare for the Homeless Board. Through the years I benefited from the wisdom and guidance of inspiring mentors. I thank you Charlie Blythe, Jene Galvin, Steve Elliot, Bill Faith, Sheila Crowley, Brian Davis, Jim Cain, Gordon Packyard, John Donahue, Anita Beaty, Bob Erlenbusch, John Parvensky, John Lozier, Jeff Singer, Rita Markley, Barbara Anderson, Michael Stoops, Hugh Grogan, Mary Ann Gleason, Fred Karnas, Joel Segal, Phil

Papas, Lynn Lewis, Paul Boden, and Peg Moertl. I also benefited from diligent and dedicated staff members and colleagues. Thank you for your patience: Barbara, Brad, Michael, Lisa, Nick, Ian, Bob, Christina, Judea, Brent, Ivy, Candace, Mick, Dorothy, Claudette, Marie, Gwen, Jennifer, and all the interns who passed through the organizations. These organizations gave me a chance to rise up and make a difference in the world.

A heartfelt thanks to many who offered me a chance to use my artistic talents: David Mizel, Joel Davis Alphonso "Zo" Wesson, Jay White, William Alexander, Taffy Douglass, staff members at The Cincinnati Arts Consortium, CCV, City Cable, Jokers Comedy Club, Go Bananas, Ashley Talent, and all the other clubs that booked me.

My special thanks to Terry Richards and John Briggs for their amazing editing.

Finally, if I missed anyone, please do not be offended. Charge it to my head and not my heart.

Chapter 1

At the Beginning…the End

Dear Donald (past),

I was nervous. Second guessing and self-degradation were the voices shouting the loudest during one of the most exciting professional engagements of my life. Old habits and self-doubts die hard. My enemies, fear and hopelessness, followed me here. Instead of being proud and enjoying the moment, there I was going down a mental checklist of why I, Donald Whitehead, had no legitimate business at the house of a former President of the United States. Sure, I reasoned, I could be there as an interloper, kitchen help, or an intruder given seconds to explain myself before being swiftly escorted out by secret service. However, reality sunk in, I was invited, I was not there as an imposter, and people were treating me as if I belonged. Donald Whitehead was "on the list."

I was not dreaming or living a hallucination. Still, the photographer's response surprised me. I did not expect anyone to want a visual record of my attendance at the event or to give me an option to request my own record. But, there the photographer was explaining to me how many shots he would be taking, assessing problems I might present for the shots, and then disappearing, without further interaction until weeks later when I ordered pictures.

Next, a 20 something male staffer asked if the information they collected was correct, including the pronunciation of my name, which I thought was obvious. Satisfied, he headed for the next guest, and his place was taken by another staffer (apparently half the people in Washington are on someone's staff). This staffer, dressed in khaki pants, white shirt, and a navy blue blazer, placed his hand on my shoulder and gently guided me to an appropriate position, as well as giving me the protocol for what was about to happen: "Please don't reach for anything, and keep your hands out of your pocket." He also told me the expected wait time was up to an hour.

And I waited. Waiting is a way of life in Washington, D.C., much like the military. While serving in the Military I discovered everything takes a long time, longer than regular civilian life. You become accustomed to lines which seem to wind miles and excessive paperwork. "Hurry up and wait" is the common phrase. Living in Washington you spend hours in traffic sometimes a 30-mile ride takes two hours. Getting into Government buildings, attractions, or restaurants always requires a wait.

You learn quickly Washington is a city where important things happen, and the urgency of addressing important matters trumps everything and almost everybody. And, because of that, you learn to wait; and you learn to master the art of small talk to pass the time. I talked to the people standing next to me. They were from the Department of Labor, so we talked about jobs, poverty, effective programs, and what could realistically be done regarding legislative needs. I talked to someone behind me; she was new in DC, but had come from Kentucky, right across the river from my hometown of Cincinnati, where I lived almost all my life.

She asked about housing, the greatest concern for every new arrival. Not housing for the poor, but rather places to live, recommended locations, traffic patterns, and above all the high rent, making life in the nation's capital seem beyond financial hope.

After about twenty minutes, a more senior staffer (you learn to recognize not only who's who, but at what level people work) came out and said we would be looking at approximately thirty to forty minutes more, and we should make ourselves comfortable and not leave. The lady from Kentucky joked about who consider leaving, and I laughed, but not too much because I would have waited the whole night.

Strangely enough, the call came sooner rather than later. Yet another staffer walked out, holding a clipboard, much like a backup quarterback on a sideline. He motioned us forward, with the two people from the Labor Department leading the way and me following the lady from Kentucky. The room was a small greeting room attached to a larger office, and that office attached to the remaining areas of the house itself. As we entered, I saw the four men in dark suits move smoothly in an orchestrated pattern, heading for, and then opening a second door across from where we entered. The staffer with the clipboard put his hand on the elbow of the first of the Department of Labor people and guided him more to the center of the room. We followed and stood waiting. There were no chairs, although various pieces of furniture lined the left wall of the room under a huge mirror.

I remember licking my lips and rubbing my hands together. But it was only a minute before the men in dark suits fanned out to flank the opposite door just as yet another staffer, an even more senior person, entered through that door. He stepped to the side, as yet another man walked in. This man stood still for only an instant before he began what must have been for him a perfected litany:

"Ladies and gentlemen, please give your attention…"

The last man to enter looked like he did on television and in hundreds of pictures, although a bit taller and a bit heavier than I envisioned. He thanked us for coming, and then began what struck me as an impassioned commentary on the shame America had to feel, given so many of its citizens were poor, homeless, unemployed, or all three. He promised he would personally see to it that something was done about this disgrace.

When he finished speaking, the two Department of Labor people were introduced to him and he spoke with them for at least a couple of minutes; the lady from Kentucky (I later learned she was with HUD) received slightly less time, and then it was my turn. I stepped forward, smiled, and one thought returned: this could not be happening. Not to Donald Whitehead, not to the man who had lain on the floor of an emergency homeless shelter in Cincinnati, Ohio. Not to the man who once had been so desperate and homeless.

But it was happening. I extended my hand.

"Mr. President," the staffer said, "let me introduce you to you Mr. Donald Whitehead, the Executive Director of the National Coalition for the Homeless."

And I stepped forward and shook the hand of former President William Jefferson Clinton, and we began to speak, as if we were old friends, about homelessness in the United States of America.

Later in the evening, I had a chance to speak with Mrs. Hillary Clinton as well, and I was impressed at how knowledgeable she was about homelessness. I was astonished because she listened to what I said. Mrs. Hillary Clinton listened to Donald Whitehead, far more attentively than others listened when I was a homeless addict in the gutters of Cincinnati.

When I left the Clinton home that evening, I felt as if I was a different person. I felt as if the Donald Whitehead who left the office of the National Coalition on Homelessness to go to the Clinton home had been transformed and invigorated.

And yet, I knew in the deepest recesses of my heart and mind, I knew the truth. For I realized then, as I do now, I was the very Donald Whitehead. I realized, in fact, that I was the same Donald Whitehead sprawled the Drop-Inn Center's floor, on Twelfth Street, in Cincinnati, drunk, unable to get up, or take care of himself, just 6 years earlier.

Even as I walked away from my evening with Bill and Hillary Clinton, again and again I was haunted by memories of my nights in the Drop-Inn Center. Questions of self-reflection flooded my soul. How could the same Donald Whitehead who slept in an emergency shelter with alcohol on his breath and clothing could be invited to the home of a President and Senator? Did the hand of God reach out and, in some strange way, to choose me for the position? Or was it something I did myself? Had I found some inner strength and will power? Or was it the kindness and support of others? Was it personal attitude and commitment? Or was it good fortune, or being in the right spot at the right time? Was it fate? Was it providence? Was it strength?

Over the years, I've considered how my answers evolved since that night and tasks and challenges I've undertaken. I've had time to examine steps I initiated and steps others pushed me to take. I've thought about what I did for myself and unpredictable events. And, above all, I feel that I've learned a few things, not only about Donald Whitehead, but about struggle and desperation, and the ways that I and other individuals have faced up to these foes. I've learned about opportunity, and I have things to say about the opportunities that each man or woman has in their lives, and the role that recognizing opportunity plays in each person's success. I've learned about fear and hopelessness, too; and I have a number of things I want to say about those two enemies of the human spirit, as well.

And so, I've written this book. I've written it not only to tell people about Donald Whitehead (although I do hope you will find my story an interesting one), but also to help people see themselves. I want my story to be uplifting. I want my story to describe truthfully what I once was, and I want people to see what I became, not so that I should seem important, but rather that the possibilities for other men and women should seem important. We are all people of different skills, people of different fears, different beliefs. We are all people with many problems, and in the lowest of our moments, we are people who believe we have few solutions to those problems. I want to address those lowest moments in the light of what Donald Whitehead once was, in light of those horrible times in the Drop-Inn Center. I want to address fears in light of the terror I felt when I woke up night after night on a cold floor, surrounded by society's outcasts. And I want to address opportunity in light of the positions I have held.

But above all, I want to highlight hope. I want anyone who reads this book to know there is always hope. I want everyone who reads this book to take away from these pages a genuine belief that with determination and courage, many great things are indeed possible. No one's life is ever totally hopeless. And that is what this book is really about.

*Dear Donald (past),
Thank you for not giving up.*

Something to Talk About...

1. Recall a time when you were somewhere you never dreamed you would be. (Positive or Negative) How did you feel? What were some of your thoughts? Why did you think this was out of your reach or impossible?
2. Have you or do you ever feel unworthy? Why?
3. Can you relate to the author? What words of encouragement would you give him? Yourself?

Chapter 2

Long Ago and Far Away

Dear Donald (present),

I wish I could tell you the story of the man who was invited to the home of President and Mrs. Clinton, and introduced as a man of some importance, was my entire story. But as I've already hinted, it is in no way the complete tale. So let me begin another branch of the story: an entirely different and far less pleasant branch. A branch at the beginning.

While it may be true that one's life is never hopeless, I'm sorry to tell you Donald Whitehead, the man who hobnobbed with the Clintons, came as close to proving that statement false as any one man should ever be able to do. To understand that, we must leave Washington D.C., and travel to an earlier time: 1995 and the "Drop-Inn" Center in Cincinnati, Ohio.

The Drop-Inn Center was in a battered, faded yellow building on Twelfth Street in a poverty-ridden section of Cincinnati called 'Over-the-Rhine,' however, it could be anywhere from coast to coast in the America you and I know so well. The Drop-Inn, or "Drop," as those of us who lived there came to know it, also as being well-named. The Drop served those who dropped through each layer of society until finally hitting a bottom you should hope you never experience. The Drop served men and women for whom their ride stopped in that dingy, stinking yellow building on Twelfth Street. Their ride came to a crashing and ripping halt. The Drop serves those whom society has allowed to slide away from what we call the normal world; it serves those whom society has failed and those who have failed society and, even more, have failed themselves. The Drop-Inn Center served those who have dropped their lives into a gutter.

In 1995 and 1996, The Drop served me.

It's almost impossible to convey my memories of the Drop-Inn Center from those days; because it's hard to remember exactly what happens when you are dead drunk or so completely stoned on crack cocaine. Your thoughts have no relation or connection to your body or anything else. In 1995, the description applied to Donald Whitehead, future Executive Director of the National Coalition for the Homeless.

In the spring and early summer of that year, I lived in abandoned buildings. I lived in battered tenements whose owners had given up hopes of selling or renting. I lived in shattered shells of structures, and it was heaven to find the electricity had been left on in one of them, there was still running water, and the plumbing still worked. I lived in buildings where homeless persons built fires on the floor to stay warm (and the landlord prayed fires would catch and spread). The landlords were speculators who bought properties in emerging community and held on to them while the communities were gentrified. Once other developers invested their initial investment multiplied. The return would sometime double the initial development. During that time the community was resistant to the development. The process is a long process to begin with the protest made it a really long process some investors were ready to back out however if the building caught on fire that could collect insurance payments which paid out much more quickly. I lived in sites where every moment was dangerous and any second a crack cocaine dispute might break out and jump from words to gunfire. I lived in buildings where the stench was gagging. And yet I, and other people like me, bore it because we had little choice. After all, we were "the hopeless people," weren't we?

The people around me were dealers and heads, those who sold crack cocaine and those who used crack cocaine. I shook hands with all of them daily and although I never seriously dealt cocaine, I used it and it used me. Whenever I owned a little cocaine, then cocaine owned all of me, and I have never met an addict for whom that was not true. At my worst, I would have done anything for cocaine, hurt anyone, or betrayed anyone.

On a larger note, some of the saddest studies in all sociology show that the black community, by the early 1980's, had begun to develop and display all the trappings of a segment of society on its way up, a part of America following in the path of the Irish, the Italians, and hundreds of other immigrant groups that had melted successfully into America. Groups that had melted in and then moved up. Then came crack cocaine, and the entry of those little rocks into the black community smashed that community like no other force could have done. Not even the horrors of alcohol can match crack cocaine, and I was both an alcoholic and a crackhead.

And so, when I could not get crack, I drank. I worked almost every day while I was homeless, I worked during the time at temporary services. I worked at landfills, stadiums, and chemical factories. I worked to feed my addiction. Some nights, I would drink until I was not even aware that I was drinking. I would drink until the action of moving a bottle of rotgut to my mouth became as autonomic as breathing; until suddenly, somehow, that bottle became empty, and I was surprised by that event because I was not aware that I had been drinking. There are those who might think such a thing impossible, but I can assure you they are wrong.

And so the addict went to the Drop-Inn Center. I went not because I wanted to go to a shelter with programs, but because there were no buildings open that night or because the buildings were so dangerous even an alcoholic crackhead could see survival was uncertain. I went to the Drop for food when it was too much of a chore to go to one of the other soup kitchens or because those kitchens' food wasn't to my liking that day (a constant topic of conversation among the homeless is the day's menu at different soup kitchens, pantries, or churches). Even a mattress on the floor was an improvement over a risky fire in an abandoned building. I went to the Drop when the police did their sweeps and left people like me no choice. I went when I was simply too lazy or too far gone to find my way to anywhere but the Drop-Inn on Twelfth Street in Cincinnati, Ohio.

But I never went to the Drop for help, at least not consciously. Although almost every emergency homeless shelter in the United States offers some type of program, some way to take the very first infant step out of the muck, I never thought that I would take advantage of those programs. (Today, I am on the Board of Directors of the Drop-Inn Center, and I'm happy to say it is next to impossible to stay more than a few nights at Drop and not become involved in some serious efforts and programs to change your life). No, in those days all I wanted from the Drop-Inn each night was a mattress on the floor, in a heated building, and a hot dog and whatever else came with it before I returned to cocaine and alcohol the next morning. If all I had to deal with was self-loathing and the terror of waking up on that cold, cold floor in an emergency shelter full of people that society considered to be garbage, then what was the problem? In fact, to a crackhead and alcoholic, what could have been different?

And yet, there I was, only a few years later, in the home of a former President and a then-current United States Senator. Sometimes, as I sit and wonder about my life, I'm struck by nothing more than its breadth. There are people who are said to have experienced the lowest lows and then found the highest highs. I am one of them. It is a constant source of astonishment to me that either of those things—becoming a homeless alcoholic and crackhead, and then hobnobbing with a former President—could have been a part of my life.

Thinking back on how my life began and developed, I now recognize, from a position of greater wisdom, that those highs and lows were always with me, unseen and unknown, but there nonetheless.

Let me explain how things began.

Dear Donald (present),
Thank you for taking up the torch.

Something to Talk About...

1. Have you ever been to a Drop Inn Center? Where? Why were you there? What did you think of it?
2. The author said he never consciously went to the Drop Inn Center for help. What do you think he meant by that statement?
3. Are there any Drop Inn Centers in your city or town? If so, what services or programs do the centers offer? Do you know anyone personally who could benefit from those services?

Chapter 3

Early Family Days

Dear Grandpa,

I was born in Cincinnati, and I've always considered myself a Cincinnatian. As I ponder the time I spent with President and Senator Clinton, I turn back to my early days in that city–well before the Drop-Inn Center. One strange fact comes to my mind: it's funny, but if you asked most of the people I encountered in the early part of my life, the idea of me meeting the President of the United States would not have been hard for my friends to imagine. If you asked my teachers, coaches, fellow church members, and even my Boy Scout troop leader, all would have predicted my success.

After all, wasn't I voted most likely to succeed in my high school class? Didn't I possess charm and brains? I had some of "what it takes", right? What a twisted route it has been to success. And I understand today, because of the many studies that I have read regarding abuse, recovery, and homelessness, that both my addiction and eventual homelessness were predictable. The environmental and psychological factors contributing to both conditions were present in my childhood, even though they often seemed hidden.

My earliest memories are of the big house on Beecher Street in Walnut Hills in Cincinnati. The house was huge and, to a child, it seemed filled with secret rooms and dark hidden passages: ideal place for hide and seek. The neighborhood was a thriving African-American community with the familiar sounds and scents from the early sixties, especially music. We lived about ten blocks from a truly unique spot in Cincinnati called People's Corner (the hub of Cincinnati's African-American community at the time). I remember the tantalizing aroma of barbequed chicken from the Tasty Bird Restaurant. I remember Albert's Grocery Store where everyone shopped and chatted as if Albert's was a huge melting pot of its own. My father worked at Checker's Toy Store. It was magical. The community was rich beyond money.

We lived with relatives I called my grandparents, who were my great aunt and uncle. Nathaniel and Laura Riep were well known and highly respected in the community for their contributions to the richness of life. Nathaniel and Laura were prominent lodge members.

Nathaniel–grandpa–was a potentate at his lodge. Grandma–Nanny–was a member of the Eastern Star lodge. She was also an artist; in fact, she was the first African-American art teacher at Ohio State University.

In addition to my grandparents, my Aunt Bea (who *was* my grandmother) and my two cousins, Bea Pat and Peggy (actually my aunts) also lived with us. With so varied a household, relations and titles were more decided by stature within the family than by formality. In those days, I remember the house as if it were a little People's Corner of its own: always filled with laughter, especially from Grandpa. My grandfather (great uncle) reminded most people of the great abolitionist Fredrick Douglass, right down to a healthy head of silver-gray hair. He was an amazing man who was always willing to help me understand things. He set high standards of thought affecting me to this day. As a toddler I was curious, forever asking what was this, what was that. Grandfather always took the time to answer. I remember family picnics with him. He told us ghost stories and we played Batman and Robin. I also remember falling through my father's convertible roof. My grandfather had the spirit of Fredrick Douglass in his heart. According to my great aunt/grandmother, we are the direct descendants of Fredrick Douglass. I will investigate this claim one day.

Everything changed on Beecher Street when I was about five. One of the strongest memories I have from those days of change was a situation I brought on myself. I stuck a spoon in an electrical socket and discovered the laws of electricity in the worst possible way. Grandpa saved me, but I ended up spending a week at the Shriners' Burn Institute. I remember being scared and that fear has never left me. Electricity and burns make me shiver even now.

Going to school to take the kindergarten placement test was frightening. As a little boy accustomed to a warm and loving family with affection everywhere, the visit seemed like a trip to a hostile zoo. I was paralyzed by the stares from strangers in authority and I didn't understand. The other children were the first real people I was dealt with outside my family. I couldn't move and I failed the test although I knew every last answer. I was ashamed and mortified. Those feelings are vivid to this day.

It was 1967 and the highway came. America's Interstate System was in its birth pangs, and the new Interstate Highway ripped through the center of our community even though there was no exit. Each day we watched the highway being built and homes and small businesses being torn down. We saw changes being forced into the world we all loved. The Interstate Highway cut through the center of Walnut Hills and it turned the wonderful neighborhood into almost two different places. Life changed forever what had been home for so many people. It somehow cut the community off from itself, off from the full knowledge of what it once had been. In only a short time, it was as if People's Corner had become a ghost town.

And we moved.

The house we moved to—on Delaware Avenue—was not as elegant as our home on Beecher Street. We still lived with Nanny and Grandpa, and Bea Pat and Peggy lived upstairs, but all the kids now shared a room on the second floor. Momma and Daddy shared a room that was also the living room and then there was Miss Mary's room (another cousin) and the kitchen.

There were five of us kids by then and we were close in those days. Sherri was the oldest and she was always bossing everybody around, but at the same time, she always stuck up for everyone in her family. Carmen, my next oldest sister, was my buddy and we talked about everything, often as if we were on some special plane no one else could understand. I remember one unfortunate time when I stuck Carmen in the eye with a pencil. I didn't mean to stick her in the eye: she was looking through the keyhole and I was trying to block it with the pencil. It hadn't at all seemed to me that I could do any damage and my action was thoughtless. Daddy whipped me long and hard. Carmen was rushed to the hospital for her eye injury, and so I got the bad end of the extension cord. Extension cord whoopings were always the worst and Daddy went crazy when he was whopping you. I could have blinded Carmen.

Darrin, my next youngest brother, was my partner at the explorer level. Darrin and I had a talent for looking at something and taking it apart. We attacked radios, televisions, and just about anything else we could get our hands on. Darrin and I did everything together whether trying to understand the wonders of the console television, playing board games, and reading the paper. My sister Angie was the last of the five children. Angie, is the baby girl. She came blessed with a talent for making everybody laugh. Everybody loved Angie.

On Delaware Avenue, I had other friends and I enjoyed life at first. But, as we got older, I started to get less attention as my younger siblings took my place as the center of my mother's world, and so I made up an imaginary friend. I don't know when I began to act that relationship out; that I can't quite place, but I do know that it started as a way to get attention. I made up an imaginary friend-who lived in our wall. I engaged in long conversations with him. After a while my imagination got the best of me and I became half-obsessed with my friend in the wall. I named him David. My mother and everyone else became concerned and began paying more attention to me, which, looking back, was exactly what I wanted. My mother took me to a psychiatrist who said I had an overactive imagination which was completely normal. Thank God for that, everyone agreed. Sometimes, today, I wonder if that psychiatrist would have rendered the same decision if he had been able to see the future.

Just after that, I started school. From the very beginning, I loved school, where I quickly found I was the center of attention. Columbian Grade School was the sort of institution where everyone from the principal to the janitor went the extra mile for the kids. I was in the accelerated class (everyone had forgotten my kindergarten freeze-up), and my teacher, Ms.Little, was the sweetest person you could ever meet.

All of her students were excellent; and, in fact, a large group from that school went on to Walnut Hills High

School, the educational summit of the City's public school system, for which serious achievement was required. Ms. Little was an outstanding teacher, but there were others who helped to form me as well. Ms. Brown, the school principal, and my math teacher, Ms. Orr were very important to me, and I will never forget them.

But it was my mother who had the greatest impact on me.

My mother is the most beautiful person I have ever met. She was always there for us and, even with six children and a husband who abused her, she always took the time to show an abundance of love and caring. I can't imagine how incredibly tough it must have been as she struggled to put food on the table, and clothes on our backs even while she defended herself from years of abuse. She walked us to school every morning and, later on, she even started working in the school lunchroom. She has always been my inspiration, and it is very clear to me today that if she had not pushed each of us, if she had not constantly reminded us of the value of education, if she had not fought for us, I and my siblings would have withered under the tremendous stress of what lay in the path of our childhood.

Dear Grandpa,
Thank you for filling our house with laughter.

Something to Talk About...

1. What city and state were you born? Raised?
2. What is the earliest childhood memory you can recall?
3. The author writes about his family and extended family. Does his account remind you of anyone or something?

Chapter 4

My Father

Dear Darrin & David,

It's hard to write about my father, because what I recall more than anything else is his anger, rage, and drunkenness. Beyond that, I remember very little and I wonder if I *want* to remember.

Quite early in my life, my father was in a terrible car accident, an accident so bad it was headlined on the evening news. He wrapped his car around a tree so violently the car was warped into a "U" shape. My father survived, but not without an injury that warped him just as the accident had warped the car. His face was split down the middle and from then on Daddy was sentenced with an injury that could not be erased.

His anger, rage, and drinking intensified. None of us was ever immuned from his anger and my mother was often the target of his fists and kicks. I remember the whoppings my siblings and I endured, beatings with the cord became a part of our lives. My father's funeral was when I found out he was a former Golden Glove boxer. Perhaps is was that history of physical violence boiled over which lent itself to pain and abuse.

And I remember my father getting shot.

I remember my father getting shot by my grandfather.

My grandfather and my father never got along, but as my father's drunkenness and physical violence began to center on my mother, the toxic relationship between my father and grandfather escalated. One day, during one of my father's rages, my grandfather shot him. My father survived and for a little while, he became better, but in the longer run, the shooting only added to his pain and violence. What a traumatic memory for children to have etched in their hearts and minds! Our father was full of anger, rage, and he was shot by our grandfather.

We moved into a house on Ridgeway Avenue and the house, at least, was a noticeable improvement. The boys had a room, the girls had a room, and my mother and father had a room; and no one else lived with us. We even had a basement, and in the basement, we had a pool table. For a little while, things were not so bad. In those days I was in fourth grade. My mother was now working as a teacher's aide at Columbian, and everybody loved Mrs. Whitehead: the students, the teachers, the principal, everybody. I had moved up from the Ms. Little's class and I was still a straight "A" student, but I really missed Ms. Little (I was heartbroken when I found out that Ms. Little had gotten married. I think I had a crush on her).

As a fourth grader, I became interested in drama, and I got to play the lead character in several classroom plays, thus starting a flair for theater that remains with me today. Possibly because of my love for drama, I was popular at school and I enjoyed that; in fact, I did everything I could to get people to notice me.

I also became interested in sports. We lived a block away from the recreation center and we really got involved. All of the Whitehead kids competed on the swim team and we were pretty good. In fact, my brothers Darrin and David both won City Championships; (I qualified for the city championships, too, but finished a disappointing seventh). After that, I tried softball. I wasn't very good at first but I practiced and taught myself and eventually became a starter and then a star.) Throughout the year, our house was filled with first, second, and third place sports ribbons and trophies. The Whiteheads were hot stuff, athletically.

At some point during my last three years at Columbian Elementary my personality changed for the worst. I started getting into fights. There were a few bullies in my early childhood, older kids who picked on us because we didn't have any older brothers. The neighborhood thugs always terrorized my sister, Sherri, and me. One time one of the bullies, a guy named David, was picking on my brother, Darrin, and so I hit him with everything I had. I braced myself because I knew I was going to get hit back and it was going to hurt. To my amazement, big bad David cried and ran away. After that day I stopped being afraid, at least visibly. The truth is, I was never taught to fight, but I was winning because I was so scared I always threw the first punch.

I rarely saw my father when we lived on Ridgeway. My mother started night school so the kids were under Sherri's totalitarian system. I felt sorry for Daddy when they took him away, just a little. Daddy was sent to the workhouse. I didn't know what the workhouse was but it sounded really bad.

In 1975, when I was in sixth grade, I had the most miserable year of my life. First, we moved again. Since Daddy was in the workhouse, Momma couldn't afford the house. Then, just as we were about to make that move, I had an accident and suffered a serious cut on my finger. At the same time, I developed a urinary tract infection. On short notice, the doctors decided that I needed surgery for both conditions, and I soon found myself in the hospital for three weeks.

I admitted, I enjoyed my hospital stay, although I wasn't at all pleased to learn my grandfather was ill. I was very close to my grandfather, and I was eager to get back to see him. I was certain he would perk up as soon as I came back, and I imagined us dipping toast into coffee and listening to the Reds games just as we had done so many times.

My grandfather died while I was on my way home from the hospital. I cried and cried for four whole days.

By the time I returned home from the hospital, we were moved. We now lived in the big house that we had lived in before, with Nanny. But things were clearly different. First of all, Nanny took in boarders and we had only three rooms to live in. That was all we could afford. The other problem was Nanny herself. She was a very different person from the woman she had been when I was smaller. She developed a mean streak. She did not want us there, and we were surprised and reacted badly, which only seemed to harden Nanny and to extend her bad temper. What we did not realize was that Nanny was reacting to the loss of Grandfather, her life partner. Nanny had become cruel and we failed to see that to Nanny, life had become cruel. Nanny died shortly thereafter.

And so suddenly, we had the big house to ourselves. The boarders left and we had all the floors and all of the rooms. In fact, for the very first time in my life, I had my own room. It felt strange. But there was one thing that happened that was a bright spot. I passed the entrance exam for Walnut Hills High School on the very first try, no small achievement. Walnut Hills was—and remains—an elite school in the Cincinnati system. I was surprised though, that some of my friends from Columbian did not pass. Most of the really bright kids did, of course, but it somehow seemed to me that all of the people I knew would be going to the same school, and I was surprised when that was not the case.

I was also surprised over my sister, Sherri. Both she and Carmen had no trouble passing the exam–my mother saw to that. But after passing the exam, Sherri decided to enroll in another school, a school with a decidedly worse reputation. We were all surprised. I never understood why Sherri did that, and as I prepared myself for the new school, I thought about her and the friends who would not be going with me, and I found that strange and scary.

I had no idea how strange and scary things were about to get.

Dear Darrin & David,
Thank you for helping me stay on the team.

Something to Talk About...

1. Recall a time when one of your parents, guardians, caregivers, etc. embarrassed you. (Funny or Not so Funny)
2. The author wrote about being humiliated by his father's actions and being teased. What advice/words of encouragement would you give to that little boy? What advice/words of encouragement would you give to yourself?
3. What would you say to the children teasing him? What would you say to children today who tease or bully their peers?

CHAPTER 5

Academic Highs...and Lows

Dear Mr. Terry,

I was proud of passing the entrance exam for Walnut Hills on my first attempt. Walnut Hills was both a junior and a senior high school, and I began attending in the seventh grade. The first thing I noticed was not something that was there, but something that wasn't: my mother had not made the transfer from Columbian with me: I was on my own. And that was not good.

From the very first day that I stepped through the doors of Walnut Hills, I felt different. To start, I was intimidated by the sheer physical size of the school. It was bigger than any place I'd ever been in my life. The classes were still easy for me, although I discovered everybody was just as smart as I was. At Columbian, I received more than my share of the attention by being the first to finish a test or the first to answer a question. Now other people finished at the same time or sooner and other hands shot up to answer a question just as quickly as did mine, so now I needed a new way to get attention.

Football was that way. At first, just as with softball, I was no star, and in fact, I was kicked off of the seventh grade team for goofing around during practice. Still, although I was raw and knew little about football, I was confident that I would someday be a player. I tried other things: I worked on the Eagle's athletic service at games and got to know a lot of the varsity football and basketball players. My social studies teacher, Mr. Terry, was the basketball coach and he asked me to be the manager of the varsity basketball team.

Being the manager gave me instant popularity with the varsity team, and as a seventh grader, hanging out with the eleventh and twelfth graders gave me a chance to become very popular with my classmates. I idolized the older ballplayers and they were nice to me. I also gained a new love for basketball and sports in general, a love I carry with me today. In the eighth grade, I not only made the junior high school team, but I started both ways, and the next year, I made the freshman team. We were undefeated for both of those years. I also made a lot of friends, too many to name, some of whom are still with me today.

I was popular. I was an outstanding athlete at a time in any young person's life when sports stardom is a huge thing. And yet, I still felt inadequate. For one thing, this was the first time in my life I felt poor. So many of the kids at Walnut Hills came from well-to-do families, and the difference was a real shock to me. My classmates drove nice cars and lived in nice homes and we didn't have those things. Once upon a time it didn't matter but now it did. It mattered a whole lot. In an attempt to make more of myself, I found and developed another skill: the funny bone. I became the class clown. Not, of course, in the way that some people did, because those people were poor students with nothing else, but rather because I discovered I had a way of saying things that people found to be funny. In no time at all, I found that my humor could draw a crowd, and that was what I really wanted.

But all of us at Walnut Hills got something that none of us could have wanted: a teacher's strike, an event that cost me and many other students dearly. To this day, I truly believe that the teacher's strike at our school robbed our young hearts and minds. We counted on our teachers, and suddenly they were gone. Most of us hardly knew what that meant, but then, for what seemed like forever, we had substitutes and some classes were not even held. I, and other students, developed bad habits. Since we weren't having classes in first bell, I started skipping first bell and going to school late. By the time the strike was over, I was convinced school started for me one bell later than for everyone else, and I never really got back in the habit of making it to first bell, even though it was math, my favorite class. And so, for the first time, I ended up failing a class and having to attend summer school to make it up. Not an outstanding start.

The teacher's strike had some other effects as well. Because students suddenly had free time, we started to party during what we considered our "off" hours. Things were not good. There were fights, confrontations, disputes and, above all, very little learning. During one of those skipped periods, I had my first sexual experience, and I got drunk for the first time. I was trying to impress people, drinking Mad Duck 20/20, and my body kept trying to send me a message but I wasn't in a mood to listen. My body kept saying "this isn't what you really want to do," but I wouldn't listen; I remember I got pretty sick and I threw up all over the place. Looking back, I certainly do wish I had listened to that message my body was sending me. After that first time, whenever somebody was throwing a party, I was there and I was drinking. Or I could go over to my sister Sherri's house, where she was living with her boyfriend. Sherri gave birth to her first baby, and even with a baby in the house, I could still drink. And I did.

But at the same time, something good happened. About the time I entered the eighth grade, a family moved next door named the Thurmonds. The first time I ever saw the two Thurmond brothers, they were throwing rocks at our two dogs, Cocoa and Lobo. I took a BB gun and went out on the porch and they made a run for it. Then our mothers started to spend time together, and soon enough, it became a natural thing for me and the two Thurmond brothers to spend time together as well. The Thurmond brothers–Anthony and Michael–became as close as blood relatives. And they stayed that way from the time they came until adulthood. A lot of my friends moved away, and that had always bothered me, but now I had some friends who were staying. We became one big family; we went to church together, we went on picnics, we fought together, and we played together. We were inseparable.

In my life at that time I had another positive occurrence. My uncle, Markie, came to live with us. Markie was my father's brother, and although he possessed some of my father's characteristics, he also had some very fine traits. Markie's real name was Joseph, but everybody called him by the nickname. Markie taught us a lot more about baseball and football and boxing than I had thought needed to be learned. He would go with us out into the neighborhood, almost as a coach while we played against other kids. We went to various sporting events with him, watched games and listened as he explained in great detail what was happening. With my uncle, Markie, and the Thurmonds, life was in some ways golden.

The problem in those days was not only the events that came about, but a pattern was established itself: a sort of emotional boom and bust cycle for me. There was the boom or high times of passing the Walnut Hills test on the first try and then the bust cycle or low times and fall out from the teachers' strike. Next the boom times of making the football teams and having the Thurmonds as permanent new friends and Markie as my uncle, then on to the bust time of drinking and developing a pattern of excess.

Unfortunately, the next cycle in the pattern was back to "bust."

The partying, the good times, and the fighting had their inevitable effect on my schooling at Walnut Hills. I, who had passed the exam on the first try and had always prided myself on my mind –I had failed math and English. If I wanted to continue at Walnut Hills, I would have to go to summer school and take two other classes. Moreover, we would have to pay for the classes, ourselves–no small thing for my family. That day, my mother came to me and asked what I wanted to do–did I want to take the classes, especially a summer school Latin class, or did I want to transfer to Western Hills High School, another spot in the Cincinnati Public School system, but one a lot lower on the academic rung? My answer was obvious. Why would I want to spend a perfectly good summer taking, of all things, Latin? My choice was easy. I was off to Western Hills instead of facing the academic music.

And so, the next fall, I started the year at a new school, Western Hills High School. Western Hills was a predominantly white school–just as Walnut Hills had been, although there were also a few Indians. But it was at Western Hills where I experienced racism for the first time. I had a few friends there and, in some ways, things were acceptable, but I was raised colorblind and it was now a huge shock to be called "nigger" when I stood at the bus stop waiting to go home. I learned quickly the west side of Cincinnati was a different place.

But there were some good things at Western High, and of these the two most obvious things were drama class– which I greatly enjoyed, and…girls. Before that, I dated more or less in a circular fashion. I dated girls I knew or my sisters' friends. Michelle Davis was by far the prettiest girl, and I also went out with Beverly and Juanita, my sisters' pals. But at Western Hills, I was a sophomore, and soon enough, I started dating outside of the friends of the family arena. And, to me, it was serious dating, not the playfulness of friends that it had been closer to home. My first high school girlfriend was Felicia, who taught me a lot about dating and who remained the love of my life, until I finally met the real love of my life at a much later date.

The dominant theme of our dating was the "house party." I don't know who came up with the idea of having house parties but I know we tried to perfect that idea. Our first party attracted dozens of people, and the entire concept took off from there. Everybody loved the idea of the house parties, and things got…partier and partier. In fact, by the time I graduated from Western Hills, literally hundreds of people had been at one of the Whitehead house parties, and we were, in fact, actually charging admission and selling drinks. Needless to say, we were well ahead of our times.

Unfortunately, I was well ahead of my times in a few other ways as well. Our parties were so popular that it was only a matter of time before alcohol got to be a big thing in my life. All of us had multiple girlfriends…and we all drank like fish. By the time I reached the eleventh grade I was a full-blown alcoholic. As I drank and drank, I experienced blackouts, hangovers and all the other things normally experienced by drinkers twice my age. In the wrong way I was growing up too fast.

Alcohol wasn't the only thing on the menu. During my junior year, I started experimenting with marijuana. I had started playing on the church softball team and the nasty truth was that we smoked marijuana all the time. We played in a church league, and we were the youngest team in the league but also one of the best. We were "The Pirates," and we wore our Pirate jerseys everywhere we went. My older cousin Ed, or big Ed as we called him, came to live with us and he became another role model for me, one I wished I followed more closely. The guys at Christ Emmanuel Baptist Church, the church that sponsored our team, would be some of my longest lasting friends, and I included Joel Davis, Bro Hicks, Anthony Brumfield, Allen Davis, Anthony Cunningham, Ronnie McMullen, and the Dangerfields–David, Anthony and James–as being a big part of my life. We partied a lot and we partied hard; we played softball a lot and we played that just as hard. And to our minor credit, we also prayed hard, probably in an effort to overcome on Sunday all that we had done the week before. Monday through Saturday, we were less than perfect, but on Sundays, we made some powerful noise for the Lord in the choir stand, marijuana aside.

I appreciated the members at the church, and to this day, they were some of the finest people I met. The deacons at the church, especially Deacon Thurmond–my friend Mike's father–were outstanding and they really took a tremendous interest in the young people, taking special care to see to it we felt welcome at the church. Mrs. Thurmond was like a second mother–as well as being one of the world's best cooks–and to this day, she always calls me "Sugar." The entire Thurmond family played a big role in my personal growth and development and I am grateful to them.

Besides the Thurmonds, Jimmy Bell–our softball coach– was a tremendous person, always encouraging us to do our best on the field and in the world (Coach Bell had no idea of my marijuana problem). And Deacon and Mrs. Davis had the biggest house I had ever seen, a beautiful mansion. Their son, Joel, was a tremendous singer, whose voice sent chills to everyone who heard him. Joel was also the quarterback on our neighborhood football team, and he was smaller than many but tougher than most. In fact, those teams were legendary in urban sports. We played against older kids, but we did well, and were considered to be "league champions."

Given everything, the move to Western Hills High School had some downs and good points as well. If it was the first place that I experienced genuine racism, it was also the birth of my love of drama, and the start of my real social life. If it lacked the academic punch of Walnut Hills High School, it had sports and, I now regret to say–the parties. When you added in the effect of Sundays at the church (never mind–for the moment–the other six days), and the overall love all of us felt from the leaders and the people in the church, you would have had to say things were going reasonably well.

But, of course, that wasn't really the case.

Dear Mr. Terry,
Thank you for seeing something in me and
giving me my first shot as a manager.

Something to Talk About...

1. The author wrote about being proud of passing the entrance exam on the first try for the top public school in his hometown. What do you think this says about his academic ability? Explain.
2. What are your memories about your education for the middle school/junior high and high school?
3. The author wrote about Jimmy Bell, his softball coach, "as always encouraging us to do our best on the field and in the world". Can you recall someone (an adult) who was a positive influence on you during your formative years? Describe what you remember and how this made you feel.

Chapter 6

Academic Losses

Dear Mr. Gene Galvin,

Life seemed reasonable at our house, at least from the outside, however, on the inside just the opposite was true. My father's drinking grew progressively worse. Every night he staggered into the house and cussed everybody out or picked on one of us for no reason. We were frequent victims of Daddy's uncalled for whoopings and the whoppings became more and more violent. My father beat us with boards, switches, pine tree branches, or anything within his frantic reach. People in the neighborhood were eyewitnesses of my father's drinking habit and abusive behavior. Looking back, it's hard to see how anyone missed his drunken escapades.

One night Daddy drove home so drunk he missed the driveway by a few feet and he parked o n our front lawn. He stumbled out of the car and passed out. Yes, our front yard was a stage and Daddy was in the spotlight. The next day we played a baseball game against some neighborhood kids who saw the show in our front yard. Every time it was my turn to bat, they sang "Daddy's Home." The other team's taunt had nothing on the familiar "batter, batter swing". That day was one of the most humiliating days of my life.

Things came to a head at our house one evening when Daddy came home even more drunk than usual and went straight to his room. Minutes later I heard Momma screaming, "Stop, Donnie, stop, Donnie!" and I heard a lot of thumping and struggling as if something really horrible was going on. I don't remember ever hearing the beatings before, or maybe I chose not to hear them. But by that time, I had found a summer job, and I felt as if I was the man of the house. As I heard those awful sounds, I knew I had to do something. I was terrified of Daddy but he was hurting Momma and I knew I was the only one who could do something.

And so I did.

I went downstairs and I burst into the room. My mother was lying there, and her face was bleeding. I asked Momma what was going on. Momma said "Nothing baby, everything is alright." My father shouted "Ain't nonna yo' damn business what going on. You better get yo' ass outta my room for I beat yo' ass." I didn't move. I asked Momma, "Did he do that to you?" Daddy started laughing, and then said, "What do you think, you the man of the house now? You better get your ass outta here."

My mother started crying, and for me that was when I'd had enough. I hit Daddy with everything I had and then I hit him again and again until he fell and I jumped on top of him and kept on swinging. When I did that, the whole rest of the family ran in and started hitting him and I was screaming, "You ain't never gonna hit my mother again! You hear me, you ain't never gonna hit my momma again." In the meantime, my sister, Angie, called the police. They came shortly after, and my father was off to the workhouse again.

But just as things were changing within my family, so were things changing outside of the house for me. The biggest change was that I was off to yet another different school. Western Hills had a few qualities I liked, but far too many that I disliked, and, in some cases, even hated. The worst, of course, was being called "nigger," but there were other problems as well. My mother's solution was Hughes High School, an inner-city institution, known as either the best or the worst.

One nice thing about Hughes was that I could be in something called the City-wide Alternative Program. It might have sounded bad in name, but in fact, it was a great offering for me. The idea of the program was to give you hands-on experience, and my hands-on experience came under the direction of a man named Gene Galvin, who taught both Psychology and Political Science.

Through one portion of Gene's program, I got a chance to go down to City Hall and even to testify in front of Cincinnati Council. The case was a neighborhood discrimination issue, and we were helped by a local councilman named Jerry Springer (who would, of course, go on to other things). This was the very first time in my life I became aware of political issues–or even seen anything like what I was watching at City Hall. All around me, everything I saw amazed me. I was fascinated and a seed was planted.

Unfortunately, alongside the city-wide classes, I took other classes at Hughes, classes in basic learning skills. I was bored to death in those classes. At Walnut Hills, we worked at an accelerated level, and in comparison, the classes at Hughes were not academic challenging. My perfection of the art of being the class clown was my way to bypass boredom. I did whatever I could to get attention, everything from singing in the hallways and on the bus to wearing a diaper to school on Baby Day.

My antics worked. I became very popular at Hughes, popular enough to be the Homecoming Prince my junior year. I was also voted class vice-president. Most of the students at Hughes lived in my neighborhood which made it easier to win popularity contests.

Now I will say, I was technically a good student ... when I went to class. I did go to class enough that I was appointed as the school representative for the City Wide Government Forum, which was something I found of great interest. It was a week-long project during which we looked at city problems and envisioned solutions. As the week progressed for all of the young men and women chosen for the program, leaders were selected from each group to compete to be mayor for a day. I was proud that I made it to the final step and was elected councilman for a day. I knew that I had been matched against students from all over the city and I also knew that my school was looked down upon, as were most of the public schools except for Walnut Hills High, and so I felt that I had done my school proud.

And then something happened that was actually to have a good effect on my young life: I took PSATs and, for once, I tried to do my very best. The result was a surprise even to me: that year I scored in the 1400s (on the old style scoring system), which was outstanding in the entire city and sensational for the Cincinnati public school system. I was suddenly a serious academic talent and in no time at all, I started getting letters from colleges and universities all over the country. I was surprised and pleased.

But even though I was surprised and pleased with my test results, I still felt a desperate need for attention. And soon enough, something that had started for me even at Western Hills began coming to the forefront. I found there was yet another way to be seen, heard, and appreciated: performing. As my interest in music and drama increased, I got a chance to perform in several plays at Hughes and also in the Merry-Go-Round. The Merry-Go-Round was a talent show that displayed Cincinnati talent, and I can safely say, the talent was incredible. I worked–or wanted to work– next to groups like the "Back Stabbers" who later became "The Deele" and sold millions of records; individuals like David Mizzell and Joe Stonestreet who sold even more millions of records with the group "Blackstreet," and Joel Davis who has written songs for Anita Baker and Levert and many other groups. Being in the Merry-Go-Round was the top of the line, and I was shocked to find myself there.

Unfortunately, I learned something about my talents pretty quickly: I learned that I had a fine voice, but also nerves of cotton as a solo singer. When my turn to perform came, all I can say is that my voice was there but my nerves were not. It was embarrassing. My role as a class clown helped me get through my performance, and in fact, most of the people thought it was a joke. A ballet dancer was working behind me and she fell during the routine, and somehow people connected to my performance, thinking the two were together and that was an even bigger laughter. There was only one person not laughing: me. I was crushed and I wanted to die. Unfortunately, instead of dying I turned to my old friend in the bottle and soon the pain was gone.

Then I plummeted from the wild success of my PSAT scores back to the road to hell. The strange thing was I loved my senior year. My popularity would continue as I swept the awards. I was the Homecoming King, The Prom King, Mister Senior, Most Witty, and Most Likely to Succeed. I was also Vice–President of my senior class. I was pretty good in football for a while, until I kicked off and the ball went backwards. After that, the coaches were really rough on me, so I quit the team. I became the team mascot during basketball season, which was a lot of fun, a lot of really silly stuff. My senior year was great.

And I kept right on drinking.

But even as I drank, I still managed some other things. My sister, Sherri, got me a job at Antonio's Pizza as a short order cook. The concept was simple: she worked the front counter as a clerk while I cooked. What could have been simpler? What could have been simpler, it turned out was everything, because Antonio's Pizza was my introduction to the adult world; I was a seventeen-year old kid working with only adults, and I learned a lot about life (and nothing about pizza).

There was one guy in particular: "LP." His real name was Larry and to me, he was the coolest guy I ever met. Larry was about twenty years older than I was, and the world he moved in was so different from mine that I might as well have come from the moon. Larry hung out with a group I knew even then as gangsters. Somehow, I had earned enough to buy a car, and Larry had me drive him around all the time. I was thrilled to be hanging out with him, and Larry thought it was cool and funny to see to my education. The schooling LP gave me was in the classrooms of strip joints, private clubs, and "after-hours" places.

I remember one time when I drove him to a woman's house. Larry and the woman went into the bedroom for sex, and I stayed in the living room to watch television, being totally flustered as to what I should have done. When Larry finished in the bedroom, he came out and asked me if he could use my car. LP was my idol so I said "sure." Larry thanked me and then turned to his lady friend.

"Give my man here some," Larry said, and then he took the car keys and left. Next, LP's female friend did exactly as LP instructed her. It was my introduction to sex on a whole different level, and one that really got me hooked.

LP got me hooked in an entirely different way. Larry– the guy I idolized – introduced me first to cocaine and then to freebasing. At first, I didn't like it, but my distaste faded fast. Alcohol made me bold, but cocaine was on a totally different level: the ultimate high. After a bit, I even tried to sell cocaine, but that was–fortunately–doomed as an enterprise. I was my own best customer. Looking back, I have no real idea as to how I ever managed to graduate from high school. Homecoming King, Prom King, Mister Senior, Most Witty, and Most Likely to Succeed were all overshadowed by most likely to be drunk and most likely to be high. Yes sir, I was on my way.

Dear Mr. Gene Galvin,
Thank you for showing me the way to
political and community involvement.

Something to Talk About...

1. Have you or someone you know ever witnessed trauma in your family as a child? What coping skills did you develop? Good? Bad? Where did you learn those skills?
2. The author recalls how through his "desperate need for attention" he discovered his talent for singing and being on stage. Describe what you discovered when you desperately searched for ways to fulfill a need (attention, love, etc.) What need caused you to search?
3. What was your first job as a child/teen? Recall some of the lessons you learned.

Chapter 7

College? The Military? Two for the Price of One

Dear Leonard Romney,

I was on my way to was College: the University of Cincinnati. Given I had what looked on the surface to have been an outstanding senior year (unless you counted "LP," cocaine, and alcohol), I approached college with some confidence. In fact, I planned to take a heavy load of courses and to graduate in three years. I also planned to walk-on with the football team and to participate in drama. In addition to all of that, I now wanted to work even more hours at Antonio's Pizza. It might have sounded tough, but what could have been easier for the guy voted most likely to succeed?

Well, almost anything, as it turned out. To begin, I signed up for twenty-seven credits, a load that would have taxed a top-flight student who wasn't trying out for football and wasn't working at Antonio's. Looking back, I can only think that the cocaine gave me an added belief in my powers, a belief that in no way reflected reality.

However, something else quickly became a reality for me: the "Rhine Room." The Rhine Room was the most accessible of the local pubs—the fastest and easiest way to get beer at the University of Cincinnati, your beer parlor away from home. I was their best customer. In fact, I found myself "stopping off" for a pitcher between classes, first one, then again, and then as a regular thing. I quickly discovered I wasn't even close to making it to the next class at all. The stop for a `` cold one" rapidly became a long-term stop. And needless to say, the football coaching staff was hardly impressed with a walk-on tailback that had a tendency to show up drunk. They quickly informed me that my services were in the "no longer required" category–don't call us and we won't be calling you, either. So much for football, I drank my way off the team.

So much for working at Antonio's, too, by then, I was working pretty close to full-time (the Rhine Room wasn't free!). The job put more and more stress on my days in college, and that, in turn caused more and more stress on the job itself. One day, my boss and I got into an argument, and he ended up with his desk overturned on him (I wish I could say my action was an accident). Goodbye to Antonio's and probably no letter of reference, not that I'd ever planned to be listing pizza-making as my most significant accomplishment.

In a short time, I had completely done in my college career. I spent more time in the Rhine Room than in any of my classes; I'd drunk myself out of football and drama class, I had no job and thus no income, and, oh yes, I had done miserably in my classes, which, of course, was the expected result given that I had attended class less than forty percent of the time. Most likely to succeed had come down to most likely to be kicked out, and in record time, given the ability I had brought to the University of Cincinnati. I promised myself that I would study hard, work hard, and do well, and I had accomplished the exact opposite of what I had intended. What, I asked myself, happened? How did it happen?

Did it matter how this fiasco happened? The overwhelming matter was it happened. I came to the University of Cincinnati like an eagle with golden wings and was leaving as a ruptured duck. I was embarrassed. Since I was now unemployed and unschooled, I suddenly realized I had to find something to do. Whatever it would be, I had to find it fast.

One day I was watching television with my good buddy, Mike, we saw something interesting. We saw an opportunity to "see the world," and that sounded good to us, two outstanding young men with nothing to do. (Mike was not interested in college. He decided to go straight into the workforce.) We started imagining ourselves on the beaches of Spain and Brazil, and enjoying the high life in glamorous cities like Paris and London. We saw ourselves as young gentlemen of leisure, meant to enjoy the good life we had so justly merited. We saw ourselves as everything we could hope for, with the exception of the one thing we were somehow missing in the overall picture: to see the world, we first had to join the United States Navy. Sailors first, tourists second. We must have missed that part.

We went down and took the entrance exams, telling everyone that we would be enrolling on the buddy system. The initial entrance exams were easy, and I even did very well on the advanced tests; so well, in fact that I was offered my choice of any number of programs, including the Navy's serious nuclear program. The nuclear program, however, required another test of its very own, and I'm sorry to say that I arrived for the test almost hung over. Needless to say, Navy Nuclear and Donald Whitehead were not a good mix that day. I ended up in the Strategic Weapons System Electronics course instead.

I was signed up for the United States Navy. But something bad happened before I could get to boot camp:

my good friend, Mike, my "Navy buddy to be" decided to stay on shore. So, I entered the service of my country entirely on my own, which was unsettling. Although, surprised to say, I liked boot camp. First of all, for some reason I was in a special company—one that was excused from all the rifle drills that the other future sailors had to do. And secondly, I was the Company Yeoman, which meant that I kept the company books and acted as the company clerk. It was a really good job for someone with my skills and it gave me a chance to get the news about an upcoming event before anyone else did.

After about three weeks, there was to be a tryout for the "Bluejacket Choir." Aha, I thought, I might have had nerves of cotton regarding standing out there and singing all alone and competing with professional quality talent, but the Bluejacket Choir? I could sing, couldn't I? So what else could stand in the way? Apparently nothing, at least for the moment stood in the way. I tried out for the choir and was an instant hit. I loved the choir even more than I loved the Yeoman's job. It turned out that the choir was the only unit that got to travel off base during boot camp. Travelling off base and not having to do drills with rifles was a hit with me. We took two trips, I sang, and things were great. I recall our trip to Wisconsin. We sang at an event for retired Military Officers. It was a very ceremonious event. The attendees wore Naval Dress Uniforms and the women were formal gowns. I remember thinking how elegant it was. I was proud and happy to be a part of the choir. In contrast, I thought of the guys at the base doing the mundane daily activities of boot camp life, polishing shoes and belt buckles, or practicing folding clothes the Navy way. "Anchors Away' and Amazing Grace" are among the songs we sang I was a baritone and I was also one of three finalists for the solo for Amazing Grace.

I also used the off-base opportunities to get in a little drinking.

But when we returned from our trips, I was sadly reminded of something that had eluded me so far: I was a member of the United States Navy. Although I was an expert drinker and a fair singer, I soon learned I couldn't tie knots at all. The U.S. Navy is big on knots. Knots, it turns out, keep things on the ships from coming apart. The Navy is even bigger on not having their ships come apart. I also couldn't do beds. No matter how I tried, I couldn't make a bed "the Navy way." In no time, at all, in the mind of my company commander, I became a serious threat. Soon enough, he began sending me to the sick bay whenever there might be an inspection: he planned on taking no chances about having me around. I might have been able to sing for my supper, but I couldn't tie a knot or make a bed to save my life. I became frustrated. The company commander was an aloof kind of guy who mirrored all the stereotypes about boot camp commanders: he was loud, tough, insensitive, and concerned with me as a threat to his reputation.

Now, in boot camp you are not allowed to have your own opinions. You do everything the Navy way and only the Navy way. You do not have any opinions about anything. Except I, of course, had the opinion those rules didn't apply to me. Soon enough, I was at odds with my company commander, and things began to go from bad to worse. The simple truth was ever since the altercation with my Dad, I had a problem with authority. I could barely handle boot camp after the feud with my company commander. The choir and the yeoman's job helped just enough, but without them, I never would have made it. In fact, I barely made it at all, and I left with some bad feelings about the U.S. Navy and some serious blows to my already fragile self-esteem.

Something good came out of Navy boot camp at the

end; my family drove up to see me graduate. And to my surprise, almost my entire family–and more–made the drive from Cincinnati: my mother, my grandmother, my brother Darrin, my sisters Carmen and Angie, and even a couple of friends, Juanita and Brenda, made the trip. And my father came, too. All of this was really important to me: it was the first time that I could remember that my parents had been able to watch me participate in anything together. I was touched by the show of support and by seeing my father sober for the first time in a very long time. Suddenly, seeing my parents getting along was wonderful, and the U.S. Navy wasn't all bad. My dreams were coming true. I left for my next assignment with a great deal of optimism.

I was still assigned to The Strategic Weapons School of Electronics, and I quickly learned that SWSE was a major factor in the United States Navy's Submarine Warfare planning. What that meant to me was that I reported to the Submarine Warfare School in Groton, Connecticut. I have to say right off that I reported with enthusiasm. The visit from my family and friends was a good effect on me, especially with the change that I hoped I was seeing in my father. In addition, as I learned, I was one of the few minorities selected for Submarine School, which made me even more determined.

Yes, I was determined for a while.

The problem was I found school to be a little boring. I admit, I made some good friends there. Some came over from boot camp with me. One friend in particular named Leonard Romney, was from St. Thomas in the Virgin Islands. He had 9 brothers and sisters. We met in bootcamp. Leonard was a very gentle soul with a Jamaican accent. He reminded me of Tim Duncan the basketball great. He was a very kind person and a great conversationalist. He didn't drink or smoke and was just a great person. Leonard was also someone that the other sailors would sometimes pick on because of his accent. I felt it necessary to defend him.

Overall, I found Submarine School slower than I was used to, and soon enough, I skipped the voluntary study classes in the evenings, and hung out instead. As always, I made other new friends; friends who also were less than seriously interested in class work. And as I started to go around with these people and to spend more and more time away from my studies, I met up with some other old "friends," friends such as Bacardi, Colt 45, Remy Martin, and Seagram's, and it wasn't long before these old friends put me "under water" at Submarine School, and not the way the Navy intended.

As I started to drink again, the instructors in Sub School pretty quickly noticed the change in effort and achievement, and assigned me to mandatory night study sessions. This worked for a short time, but also had a detrimental effect in that I would leave the evening classes and head straight for my old friends; in short, I merely started hanging out at a later hour in the evening and came back to my barracks at a much, much later hour at night, or rather, morning.

Two weeks before graduation, I was told that I would not graduate with my class; I was to be recycled to the next class. I would have to do everything all over again. I was shocked and really hurt because I saw Leonard and some of my earlier friends leaving for the next stop in their SWSE training. For a little while, though, I did make an effort to do better, but soon enough, with my successful friends gone, I turned to my old friends—the one you bought off the shelf in the local liquor stores. I started classes all over again, and, even while drinking as much as I did, I was still capable of performing at a reasonably high level, mainly because I had already covered much of the material. But one day, my tenure at Submarine School came to a screeching halt.

Dear U.S. Navy,
Thank you for helping me make it through Boot Camp.

Something to Talk About...

1. Did you know what you wanted to do after completing high school? Explain.
2. The author wrote…"something good came out of Navy boot camp." Recall a personal situation, circumstance, or experience that may or may not have seemed favorable, but something good came out of it in the end.
3. Reflect on a memory from your home life, education, work, or social life during the early years of your life. Do you see any triggers which may have led to your addiction, low self-esteem, anger, or feelings of shame?

Chapter 8

I Attack the U.S. Navy

Dear Christine,

I don't remember the exact events from the night before I got into my first (and last) serious trouble at Submarine School. If I were to remember, I suppose I would see myself doing what I had done so many nights before. Probably, we went to the base PX to buy liquor, most likely two or three bottles, and it would be a very well-educated guess that we drank until the early hours of the morning, or perhaps even later. In fact, it's even possible that we stayed out all night drinking because one thing I do remember is when we got our wake-up call the next morning, I couldn't stand up. I remember how badly the room was spinning and how the entire world was somehow tilting first in one direction and then in the other. It was like one of those rides at the amusement park, the ones that spin you around like a top, but then the floor drops out and you're suddenly stuck tight to the wall, without any feeling of security at all, as if you have no idea of where you really are or what might happen next.

All I can say is I felt worse, much worse. I felt so bad that I committed one of the cardinal sins of training in any U. S. Navy facility: I went outside without my cover. Now, to those unfamiliar with the military way, and especially the Navy way, your "cover" is your hat. If you are outside, alive, and breathing, then you must wear your "cover." I wasn't.

I don't remember exactly why I wasn't wearing my cover. I suspect I was just so disoriented, so drunk I forgot it. I more than likely never even had enough presence of mind to think of it, which is no mean trick in the Navy, because never going anywhere without your cover is drilled into you a hundred ways.

Soon enough, as I was walking to class, I was confronted with an officer, who it seemed, was having a pretty bad day.

"Where's your cover, asshole?" he shouted. His screams and rant struck me like a bowl of water in the face. I reached up, touched my head and found only my own skull. I knew right away I was in trouble. Perhaps, under a more normal circumstance, I might have overcome that trouble, might have somehow gotten past that one enraged officer, and made it through the day, the week, the month, the school. But not that day not that time, because I was still drunk. I was still drunk and still having trouble with authority, especially this authority.

I simply looked at the man for a moment, and then, while he probably waited for a terrified salute, I instead yelled at the top of my voice: "Fuck you, Asshole." As the officer stared at me in total shock, I will say one thing for myself: my natural common sense—or my natural instinct for preservation—came to the fore. I turned and ran like hell. I ran like the wind. I ran so fast, that had I been back at the University of Cincinnati and still on the football team, I might have even convinced the coach to give me a second chance. I ran so fast that I managed to lose the offended officer.

When I finally thought it was safe, I headed to my class, congratulating myself for what I was suddenly realizing was a very, very narrow escape. As I became less and less drunk, I became more and more frightened at the thought of what could have happened. I sat in class, taking in a deep breath after deep breath. I dodged a bullet I fired at myself.

Unfortunately, what I dodged was a persistent bullet. The enraged officer canvassed the entire school to find me, and while Submarine School was no small place, it certainly wasn't big enough to hide me from a man willing to spend his every moment looking for me. Even though I was carrying a 3.85 average in my coursework, I was through at Submarine School, and through with special weapons as well. Moreover, to add to my embarrassment, I wasn't sent off to my next station immediately. Instead, I was tossed into a transition unit, which was a kinder term for a holding pen. A holding pen for the school's malcontents of whom I was now the new poster boy. I stayed in the transition unit for one whole month. Mostly, I cleaned bathrooms. Most Likely To Succeed, right?

Incredibly, though, I got a second chance with the U.S. Navy. It turned out because I earned such a high score on the ASFAB test; I was given the opportunity to pick a new "rate" –that is, a new training school within the Navy. I thought about it for a while, and then chose "Sonar Tech" school. In keeping with the maturity and the ability that I had already revealed in the Navy, I made that choice for an intelligent and wise reason: I chose sonar school because the school was in California. I always wanted to see California, and here was my chance! Good thinking, eh?

Actually, things started well. I enjoyed the trip to California and I still remember arriving there. One look and I knew I had made the right decision. I loved California right from the start: the climate, the food, the beaches, even the people. In fact, I loved California so much for a while I was able to focus on my Sonar School studies with renewed hope. I knew and understood I was given a second chance and one with a prestigious assignment and I was determined to do the best with that chance. Soon enough, I had gotten off to a good start in school and I was even improving in my work. At the same time, I was making new friends, and I even met a young woman from Spokane, Washington. Things were going so well for me that I couldn't believe it; it seemed like my old enemies, drugs and alcohol, couldn't find me. At last, I felt as if I was "most likely to succeed."

Of all the things suddenly going well, the most important was the young woman from Spokane. Her name was Christine Redmond, and I have, in fact, always believed Christine was my guardian angel, appointed by God to try to help me stay on the right path. She was very lovely with dark brown hair and an outstanding figure. She loved sports and she loved not only California, but the entire west coast of America. I met her on our base in San Diego where she was in Radio "A" School at the same time as I was in Sonar "A" School. We met at the Enlisted Club at RTC San Diego, RTC being the Navy's acronym for the entire training base. Christine was the kindest woman I had ever met, and formed a great relationship. We did the young lover activities, the walks in the park, the sunrises and sunsets on the beach; day after day we had fun. Christine kept me in check and happy, and with her support, I kept up my studies. I was becoming the success I always wanted to be. Christine always told me that I was beautiful inside and out and that the world was mine if I wanted it. That was always a little confusing to me. Of course, I wanted it. Christine and all loved to dance we hung out at the club until it closed and watched the stars in our secret place. It was an older building on base with a little cubby hole behind marble pillars. We could make out until curfew. I would head back to my barracks and she to hers. Our making out got more passionate each time until it was inevitable that we had to get a room. For Christine this would be her first time and I did all that I could to make it special.

Most Unlikely to Succeed

Everything was going well.

Except there was one problem. Just at a time when I was becoming more and more dependent on Christine, I was ambushed by a logistical truth regarding radio school and sonar school. Sonar school took longer: a lot longer, and what that meant was Christine finished her schooling almost before I was really getting going. She actually started ahead of me, and now the simple term of our classwork was messing everything up. And there was nothing that could be done about it. Christine was getting shipped out and things at school began to change.

With Christine's emotional help, I had been finding it fairly easy to study, and I actually carried the highest average in my class, after the first period of study. Ironically, that was when my trouble at school began. Shortly after Christine's departure and the start of our second session of studies, I scored a perfect 100 on two quizzes and I was very proud. The instructor for my class was a petty officer named Anderson. Anderson was thoroughly convinced that I was cheating on my test. I have never cheated on a test. I have always attributed his suspicion to racism; he never accused anyone else of cheating. I was disappointed Anderson would announce to the class as he passed out the test "Mr. Whitehead got a 100% on the test but we will find out how he is really doing sooner or later." People would come up and ask me how I did it. I usually laughed it off but I was very hurt. The one thing I realized about myself is that I am incredibly sensitive and what people think about me really matters.

As a result of the dual blow of Christine's leaving and Petty Officer Anderson's suspicions of cheating, I soon found myself in severe emotional waters. If Christine and I remained together, I believe to this day that I would not have gone down that path. What path? I tumbled down one of the oldest roads on the map: medication, self-medication that is. I drowned my sorrow in alcohol and the simple truth is, I drowned it all too well. I started hanging out at the base clubs alone and partying hard. Sometimes I just drank alone, but usually I was with friends or at least as a part of some group. And as I drank, two things happened: first, I forgot most of my troubles, and second, I forgot Sonar school and the United States Navy. My hard partying, and my way of handling the pressure I put on myself, would cost me dearly again.

One funny part–and there wasn't much that was in any way funny–was my singing. I always enjoyed singing from my days in the Christ Emmanuel Baptist Church Choir to the Hughes High School Choir. I had a favorite song called Fire and Desire by the Artist Rick James. In the song there is an extra loud opening note with the words "Love them and leave them". As a teenager I startled people on the school bus, at parties, and in school by belting out those song lyrics."

I always had a strong voice and I always enjoyed putting on a musical show, but I was surprised to find that I never enjoyed singing as much as I did when I was dead cold drunk. And soon enough, I invented a drunken singing game that was to prove very costly.

Apparently, I had decided that everyone on the base needed to hear me sing, and so when I returned to base, usually in the middle of the night, and always drunk, I would begin singing at the very top of my range, which was considerable, at least as far as loudness was concerned. I would sing and sing on, at the top of my lungs, waking up at least half of the entire base. And then…and then I made a mad dash for my room before anyone figured out who the drunken sailor was. After this happened a couple of times, I saw quite a few guys on the base were more than a little angry. In fact, some of them–those who were taking things seriously—were out and out furious, and eager to discover the culprit. About the only thing that was saving me was that half-asleep sailors weren't too good at voice recognition, especially when the voice was slurred over with alcohol. After I had made it to my room safely, I would often join in the next day's conversation regarding what "we" would do to "that asshole" when we caught him. Looking back, I had a death wish in those days.

But, of course, I was caught. And when that happened—as it had to happen eventually—things were pretty bad. First of all, I was caught by a six-foot-six drill sergeant, pretty much the last person in the entire world I would have picked to successfully run down the "singing sailor." I barely escaped a pretty nasty beating, but there wasn't any way at all of escaping my punishment. The next day, I was summoned to an administrative hearing—a serious thing in the Navy. The captain was furious to start and he worked his way up from there. It was obvious he believed I was a real troublemaker and it was equally obvious he had no interest is keeping me around.

Following my experience with midnight singing run my fate was written on the wall. The one thing that has been my saving grace from the time I passed my kindergarten test was my academics. I had done so well in the class that I was accused of cheating after scoring perfect scores on my previous test. Being one of the few minorities in my rating (job in the Navy) I felt that this accusation was motivated by racism. When it came to the final exam it was just the black and white numbers there was a portion of the test that required the subjectivity of the person that couldn't believe that a black person was smart enough to get a perfect score.

I compared my answer to other sailors afterward and discovered that our graph were almost identical however our scores were not. To this day I believe that either through out right racism or bias due to my behavior issues my test was unfairly scored. Perhaps the order came from up top. I am not sure, but I know, and they know that I should have moved on.

Instead I was moved out to sea as a deckhand a deckhand who had scored at the top 1% on the Navy's entrance exam. A deckhand who couldn't tie a knot. Anchors Away.

But I was gone. They kept me in a holding company for two weeks—more latrine duty—and they shipped me out to sea on the U.S.S. Horne, as a boatswain's mate, the lowest of the low. In a short time, I drank myself out of a school and training that would have been a huge leg up on a Navy career, and had instead found my way to the bottom of the barrel. On the Horne, I was assigned to the fire hose team in case of accident and to a machine gun in the case of combat. I really didn't worry about the machine gun too much, but being assigned to the fire hose team was just about the most dangerous assignment a man could get. Most likely to ….get killed?

Dear Christine,
Thank you for making my time in the Navy fun.

Something to Talk About…

1. The author recounts the time he broke one of the number one rules while serving in the U.S. Navy. He also writes about not necessarily remembering or knowing why he broke this rule.
2. Dig deep to recall a personal situation when you broke a rule. What were your consequences? Lessons learned?
3. Describe a time when you were considered a troublemaker. Was it for the good or bad? Explain.
4. "Problems with authority"---discuss how this phrase impacts your life in the past and the present.

Chapter 9

The Navy Returns Fire

Dear U.S.S. Horne 1st Division,

My journey to the fleet was rather eventful. I first traveled to the West Coast for the first time. I had never been on a plane for more than a couple of hours. My trip to LAX took about 4 hours. I have to admit I was very nervous until I found out that they had little tiny bottles of liquor on planes. Of course, I order several and soon I was fast asleep. I didn't wake up until I felt a tap on the shoulder from the stewardess it was time to land. I had to lift my tray table into an upright stance for landing. My layover at LAX was about an hour I soon boarded my next flight to Japan. Landing at the Tokyo airport was a culture shock to say the least. Japan is so colorful at least in the airport. This was my first experience with authentic Asian culture. I was so intrigued I remember wishing I had more time to explore. If Japan was intriguing nothing could prepare me for the Philippines.

The Philippines was quite confusing to a 20-year-old kid who only international travel before today was to Toronto, Canada. We were basically dropped off in Manilla and told to find transportation to Subic Bay. Subic Bay was a large Navy base in Olongapo City. We were told to watch out for suspicious looking transporters. I was not sure what was suspicious looking and what was not. My instincts told me to follow the sailors that looked like they had been there before and that's what I did. I am thankful for my instincts. It was a treacherous course a long mountain trails and jungles. It was like something out of a Godzilla Movie. I was terrified the whole time on top of the terrain and the fear that I chose the wrong transportation. I was imagining I was on a ragged bus to nowhere. To top things of the weather was bad it was storming, thunder, lightning, rain the whole nine yards. We finally arrived at the base.

My two weeks in the Philippines were by far the best times of my entire stint in the Navy. I spent most of my days sleeping into noon. I would then head out to play basketball of football. Then when darkness fell, I was off to Olongapo for the 24/7 party scene like nothing I could have ever imagined. There were pretty girls that loved American Servicemen lots of alcohol, good music and good food. I literally partied for the whole two weeks. This was paradise for a naïve 20year old. I was saddened when they told me I was flying out to Diego Garcia.

My next stop before Diego Garcia was Oman, Jordan where we transferred planes. I remember the tarmac being lined with Soldiers with M16's on their shoulders. As opposed to my stop in Japan or the Philippines, I couldn't leave Oman fast enough something felt wrong there. I remember the look of anger on the faces of the Jordanian soldiers. I didn't understand why they looked that way after all we were there friends weren't, we.

Next stop was Diego Garcia a desolate island in the middle of the Indian Ocean. I was there for several days waiting for my transport to my ship. What a contrast it was going from the Philippines to Diego Garcia. The only thing that was similar was the alcohol, there were no pretty girls, no parties and no fun. This place had beaches filled with rocks and coconuts and if that wasn't bad enough the waters were shark infested. Can you imagine looking out onto an issue layered in three shades of blue and not being able to go in the water or even get to the water without cutting your feet. There were 5 women on Diego Garcia and about 1000 men. The club was a bunch of guys listening to music and dancing in a circle. Even the beer tasted funny some of the more seasoned soldiers said it was mixed with some chemical preservative. It might have preserved something, but it did not preserve the taste.

After several weeks my journey was winding down. I boarded a transport ship and the next day I was in a helicopter headed out to my ship I thought the ship would be standing still and we would land. To my surprise we were notified shortly after we took often that we would be repelling down to the ship because it was underway. Wow now this was going to be an adventure I was terrified repelling meant me hanging out of a helicopter getting dropped down onto a moving ship! Fearful thoughts raced through my head. *What if they missed? What if the cable broke? Yikes!* Luckily, I was number 4 to repel and I was able to witness the safe execution of this seemingly dangerous activity.

Actually, at that point in time, a great many people were puzzled. The country was in the middle of the Iranian hostage crisis, and Horne had originally been on a world cruise. That cruise turned into a Middle Eastern deployment, and we set a record, sailing in circles in the Persian Gulf for a hundred and twenty-two days. I was... uh...thrilled. I was miserable. Those first three months out to sea were some of the worst times in my life. Each day was a blizzard of monotony: we painted, we scraped, we ate, we stood, we watched, we slept, and we dreamed about getting off the boat. And then, out of the steamy blue, mercy. After three months of pain and boredom, I was asked to help out the ship's journalist. To say I jumped at the chance wouldn't be an adequate description.

As a journalist's assistant, I was responsible for the ship's TV programming. I created an evening news program from the AP and a schedule based on movies and sitcoms sent from the Navy. Suddenly, I was in heaven. My intended major at the University of Cincinnati was communications and I somehow found the time to check out and even learn a little about the campus radio station. Now I was suddenly getting a chance to do something I enjoyed. From hell to heaven in a very short time. And yet, this period of time became for me symbolic of my entire Naval career: a great deal of promise and then some event that would totally transform my position.

I did well as a journalist; so well, in fact, my ship considered sending me to my third school, communications, an opportunity I would have jumped at. Then my rotation on the mess decks came up. Every new sailor is scheduled to do a stint to prepare meals, and this was my turn. My stint started positively; I was assigned to the officers' mess which was a very prestigious assignment. I did well. I prepared breakfast settings, I woke all the ship's cooks, and I cleaned the area around the captain's quarters. This was really good duty, and it had other benefits as well. It allowed me to make friends with the officers and show my maturity and ability to accept responsibility. I took a great deal of pride in my work and did an excellent job while we were out to sea. I received praise from my superiors. Things were going well both in the journalism field and my stint in the officers' mess.

Unfortunately, while I was doing well at sea, ships have a way of making port. And during the time when we had been at sea, I had accumulated eight paychecks, in those days a fairly serious amount of money. And to make matters worse, our main port of land call was Subic Bay in the Philippines, a port notorious for the opportunity to have a good time. Or a bad time. Sad to say, I took the opportunity as a chance to do myself in yet again.

By the time we docked on land, the U.S. dollar was twenty to one against Filipino currency, and that was all the motivation I needed. I hit the ground spending and, of course, drinking. At the end of the first night I was already in the brig after becoming drunk and disorderly, and being thrown in the drunk tank before the shore patrol even had a chance to charge me. On the next day, I was labeled a liberty risk, not allowed to leave my ship during the evening hours. I also missed my duty time in the officers' mess which meant nothing was set up and no one woke the cooks. As a result, I was removed from the officers' mess and placed in the dish room. But even though I was almost in a prison, I was able to overcome some of the more serious obstacles to...my drinking. Although I was a liberty risk, and thus without access to the many local bars in the evening hours, I quickly compensated by becoming adept at drinking during the day. By some miracle, I was never caught imbibing while on duty, and we only stayed at Subic for less than a month, but still, the damage was done. Once again, Donald Whitehead had managed to snag defeat out of the jaws of victory, managed to fight his way through to failure though threatened on all sides by the successes of journalism and the officers' mess.

From that time on, I was looked at as a different person by almost everyone on the ship. I was Most likely to succeed, right?

Fortunately–at least for the moment–just as a ship cannot stay permanently at sea, neither can a ship stay permanently in port. What that meant to me was that we were once more on the high seas, and thus away from convenient sources of alcohol. In a short time, I became interested once more in reading and writing, and I started reading the Bible. Soon, with the impetus of an enforced abstinence, I began to resemble the Donald Whitehead I had once been. I often wonder how things could have turned out had that status remained the case.

As the ship sailed on and then began to approach Hawaii, I was finally serene, finally on the right track, and above all, finally sober. I was working on the mess deck, though in a lesser status, and talking about what I was going to do when we finally hit land. At that moment in the mess, I was responsible for removing trays and giving them to the dishwashing crew. I had no idea trouble was approaching. As I stored my tray on the deck, a machinist's mate who was also on mess duty yelled some unsavory words at me which I chose to ignore. I have no idea what was going on with him; maybe he got a Dear John letter, or he lost a family member, two of the biggest stressors for people out to sea. Or maybe he just didn't like me. At any rate, he continued to badger me and finally he pushed a tray full of spaghetti back toward me, and my newly pressed uniform was covered with tomato sauce. When he came out of the dish room and pushed me, I retaliated by giving him a quick but severe beating in front of most of the officers on the ship.

I not only was confined to the ship during the time we were in Hawaii, but I was placed under confinement immediately, and as soon as we landed, I went to Captain's Mast, which is essentially part punishment and part trial. I lost a stripe as a demotion in rank, but even worse, I was confined to my ship for the next 45 days during which time I was also referred to an administrative hearing for a decision on whether my naval career would end early. Thus, I missed any liberty in Hawaii and, even as we sailed for and then reached San Diego, I was in confinement. For 45 days, I was trapped aboard my floating prison, and I found it unbearable.

I had one good bit of fortune, however: Christine was assigned at that time to San Diego, and so she was able to come on board the ship to see me. She stood by me in those days when I was essentially a prisoner, and I have to say that her daily visits were the only thing that really kept me going. Finally, however, I was allowed off the ship with the reminder that I had a review board date, and Christine and I had a great time in her off-hours. I knew I had the review board hearing in my immediate future and I tried as hard as I could to tone down my behavior. Possibly as a result of this, the review board did essentially rule in my favor—well, what they actually ruled was that my career with the U. S. Navy was salvageable, and they allowed me to return, although at a lower pay grade.

Thus, I had a chance to settle into what at first seemed like a normal Navy life. My ship remained in San Diego, and I had human hours and was able to live in the Navy barracks. In fact, my view of Christine as my guardian angel only grew stronger, and eventually, we became engaged and agreed to marry at the end of the year in 1979. How could I have been happier?

Well, as it turned out. While I seemed to now have something worth living for, in reality I must not have seen it that way. Within a few months, I was drinking again. I was seeing less and less of Christine because of her new duty assignments, and I used alcohol to take up the time that I was no longer spending time with her.

In no time at all, I was recommended to the Navy's substance abuse program, and, strangely enough, I can say that I had every intention of following through on that option; to some extent, I did indeed see what my life was becoming, and I admitted I needed help. But in another way, I was in denial about my substance abuse problem: I wasn't passing out like some of the heavy drinkers, and I wasn't throwing up as I saw others do. And so, somehow, in the back of my unconscious mind, I must have decided that even though I was saying the right things to people, I really wasn't in that bad a way. And the point is that that could not have been further from the truth.

If only I'd followed up with the program, my life might have taken a far different path, but ironically I was too hung-over to get up in time for the first day of the program. Missing that appointment cost me three days of bread and water in the brig and another stripe. When I got out, I was beyond caring, and the Navy was beyond caring about me. I would finally go AWOL and go to a second administrative hearing where I was found to be unsalvageable and I received an administrative discharge under other than honorable conditions.' My career with the U. S. Navy was over, and I was headed back to Cincinnati. I left so much more than stripes or military benefits in San Diego: I left pieces of myself that took years to recover. I never realized how deeply gone was the self confidence that made me "Most likely to Succeed;" gone was the moral value that was needed to keep me from falling deep into the abyss of substance abuse, and gone was Christine.

> *Dear U.S.S. Horne 1st Division,*
> *Thank you for being my friends.*

Something to Talk About...

1. The author wrote about his responsibility as a journalist's assistant. He was responsible for entertainment and news television programming

for his ship. What do think would be some good television programming ideas for the topics discussed in this book?
2. "I was able to overcome some of the more serious obstacles to…" How would you complete this statement as it relates to your life
3. What stands out in Donnie's relationship with Christine. Explain.

Donald Whitehead

Most Unlikely to Succeed

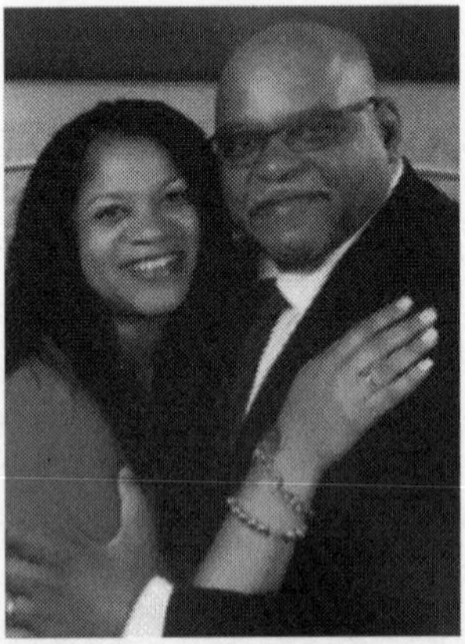

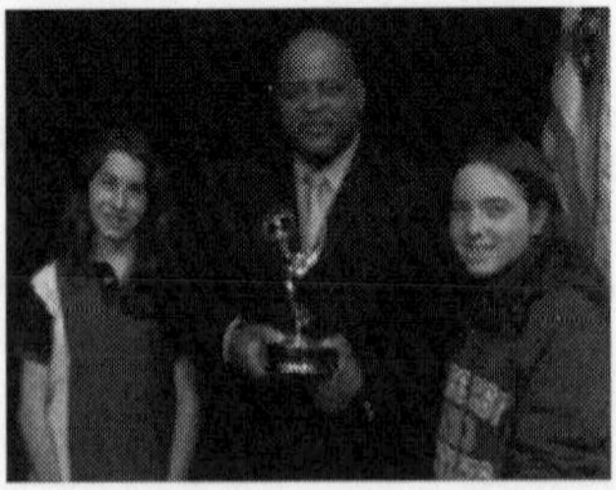

Most Unlikely to Succeed

Donald Whitehead

Most Unlikely to Succeed

Donald Whitehead

Most Unlikely to Succeed

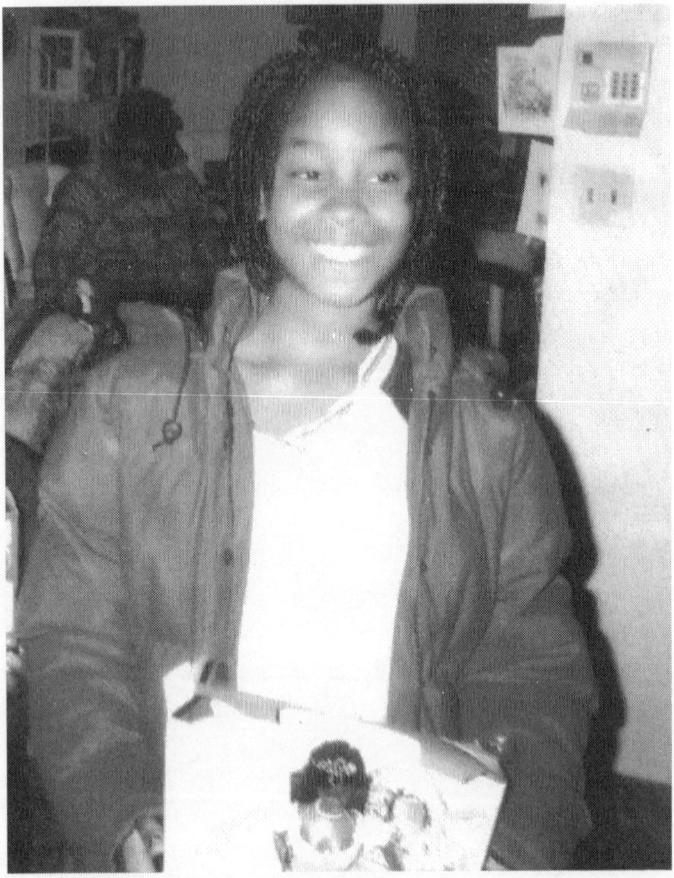

Most Unlikely to Succeed

Chapter 10

My Meet Up with Cocaine

Dear Momma,

As soon as I was discharged from the Navy, I headed back to Cincinnati and began to dig a deep hole, a hole by myself for myself. I changed, but not for the better. However, it wasn't only Donald Whitehead who changed. Cincinnati changed; it was different and in my opinion, a far worse place than I remembered when I left for the Navy three years ago. In the early eighties, the African-American communities in all of our cities were struck by a plague that could almost be described as biblical, smiting the first-born, the last-born, and all those in between. It was a plague that turned back the pages of history, a plague that rolled back many of the gains of the great civil rights leaders. It was a plague that toppled the economic gains black people started to make, and a plague that rocked every part of the world I had known, a plague that turned once-thriving communities into their very own versions of the wild, wild West. And the name of that plague was cocaine; cocaine, in its newest and far more deadly form, crack cocaine. Cocaine had been around forever and was known as a rich man's drug. In an effort to reach a different customer base (the non-rich) distributors created a concentrated, less expensive, more addictive product called crack.

My first meeting with that insidious monster took place almost as soon as I got off the bus in downtown Cincinnati, and although it would take a few years for the monster to completely ensnare me, it took very little time for me to ensnare myself. Almost from the second I hit Cincinnati, I was off to the races of self-destruction. I gave my family no explanation for what happened in the Navy, or what happened with Christine. Up to that point, I'd worked a few jobs, but none lasted past a few months or a year(?): restaurant manager, pizza delivery, short-order cook, and many I can't even remember. The new Donald Whitehead had no time for a career, family, or someone I should have loved. The new Donald Whitehead was now a man on the move. I dived head first into life, or perhaps nose first. Some friends hosted a welcome home party for me, and one of them said "try this," and produced some powder—cocaine in its new form. I tried it and then I tried it again. I thought it was great, although maybe "thought" wasn't the right word to describe what my mind was doing in those days. My strongest memory is of how my friends treated that powder, declaring "You better not spill any," as if it were gold dust I was inhaling. Little did I know, in those fleeting seconds, I inhaled, I was about to set my life back for almost a decade.

All thoughts of Christine went out the window as the powder raced up my nostrils. There was no doubt, the magic powder was the new significant other in my life. Even to this day, the decision to throw Christine away remains one of the worst I have ever made, and it will always be the source of one of my deepest regrets. She had stuck with me through all of my struggles and then I had broken things off with my behavior. Looking back, I suppose it was because I knew she would never approve of the new Donald Whitehead, the one with the fast cars, the fast life, and the fast women. Then there was the worst from this new Donald Whitehead, the fast drugs.

Technically, I got one good job. Supposedly, I worked at Jewish Hospital where the pay was good and the job was respectable. However, my one good job is not where I put my efforts because I was in "the life". I worked at Jewish Hospital whenever I was able (*scheduled?) to do so–and when I remembered to do so–and I hung out with drug dealers. Now, I wasn't a dealer, and, to this day I can't tell you what my plans were for engaging in such an arrangement. In fact, I really didn't even know my role with the dealer. Maybe I was a gofer–the lowest of the low. I never got any money, but I did get drugs– I got plenty of drugs. Yes, plenty of drugs and whatever drugs I didn't use myself, I traded for sex.

The disease of addiction is progressive and I was progressing right up until I was gradually consumed. I entered a seedy world incredibly different from the one I once knew in Cincinnati (one of our best customers for drugs, for instance, was a teacher at a high-class elementary school). What I learned during those times was that an addiction dominates everything in a person's life. The need for drugs or alcohol trumped family, church, and even life itself. And I was, in those days, completely unwilling to come to terms with the addiction I developed. I was slowly committing suicide by cocaine.

Next, of course, I became homeless. What should I– or anyone else–have expected? An addict and alcoholic, sloughing off jobs and friends like leaves? Homelessness should never have come to me as a surprise. But it did, of course. For the first few weeks and then months of my predicament, I didn't even think of myself as "homeless." In fact, I'm not even sure I really knew what the term meant.

I wasn't what most people would think of as "homeless," either. I stayed with friends, bouncing from couch to couch and floor to floor, making use of spare rooms and space in garages, making promises of partial rent and burning every bridge ever made available to me. Everywhere I went, people saw me as an addict, a user, someone to be reviled or pitied. Finally, I ran out of places to go and people to use.

There was nowhere left to go, nowhere at all. It was then my homelessness was of the more traditional variety. I slept in abandoned cars, abandoned houses, on fire escapes, in public restrooms, in parks, or wherever I could lay my head. I remember the feelings of emptiness, sadness, and loneliness. I remember sinking a little deeper, every day, into depression. One of the worst experiences about my time on the street was how other people treated me, passing me and always looking away, as if a glance into my eyes would turn them to stone. My only relief from the guilt and shame of being on the streets was the temporary grace I received from whatever drug I used on any given day. For me there was no drug of choice. I used whatever I could beg or steal. My whole life centered on getting drugs and using drugs, and then finding new ways to get and use drugs. I used drugs to live and I lived to use drugs.

Naturally, my relationship with my family was outstanding. They were overjoyed to see me plunge from most likely to succeed to most likely to be found dead in an alley. I used my family just as much as I used drugs. I concocted sob stories to get money from them only to use the money to buy drugs. In most instances, I am sad to say, I was able to get funds from my mother. It was hard to be proud of the life I lived in those days.

Thankfully, the first part of my spiritual awakening came about because of my family, more specifically, my mother. I remember it was a weekend, and I was, of course, homeless;

homeless, penniless, and craving drugs. I don't remember where I slept the night before. It could have been in an abandoned building or with a faithful friend still willing to let an addict use him for one more night. It could have been in a shelter, or it could have been that I simply slept on the streets: literally on the streets, or at best under an overpass. I have no idea if I had been high or if I had bought or sold drugs.

Now, for a homeless person, the weekends are the loneliest because there's very little to do unless you want to walk the streets, back and forth, and back and forth. That is what I was doing when I saw my mother. My mother was always there for me, but this time I was horrified to learn what she was doing: she was looking for my body. She was driving around in the worst part of Cincinnati, waiting to find me dead. I saw her and she drove over to where I was waiting. Looking back, I have no doubt I represented a picture of hell, a sight even a mother should have to love. My mother loved me. She loved me so much that when I began to try to give her a story, when I began to try to get more money for drugs from her, she said something that began to change my life: she said "no." I gave her a line (which usually worked) and begged her for money, and she said "no." My mother told me she would not help me to destroy myself. She said she had given me money in the past and I used it for drugs. She declared she would not do so now.

I was shocked. I always knew if there was any one person who would give me money, it would be my mother. Now, my mother was saying "no." This time, however, my mother was practicing tough love. She later told me it was the hardest thing she ever had to do. For me, it was the greatest gift a mother could give, although I hardly knew it or felt it at the time.

I was stunned as I watched my mother drive off. Suddenly, the realization I was truly alone in this world–with no one but myself–somehow got through to me, and it was then my life began to change. When I went back to the shelter that night, I lay down on my mat far back in the rear–away from anyone else–and cried myself to sleep, silently, because after all I was once "most likely to succeed." I cried silently that night because I was crying out for help, begging the world to somehow come to my aid, to send me the help I needed to get past the addict I made of myself. Eventually, one of the workers at the shelter came to my mat and she asked me to come with her back to the office area of the shelter. She told me she knew what I was going through, and she already knew what was wrong because she was a recovering addict herself. I told her I wanted to die because I couldn't stand living the way I was living but I couldn't stop. She said she understood and she listened while I poured out what little was left of my heart. After a while, she said was going to go into one of the offices to call a friend. Her friend, a guy named Courtney, took me to a meeting the next day, a meeting for addicts who didn't want to be addicts any longer.

Donald Whitehead, the guy who was "Most likely To Succeed" was one now of those addicts.

Dear Momma,
Thank you for saying no.

Something to Talk About...

1. The author described cocaine as a plague. Explain what you believe he means when using this description.
2. "I remember sinking a little deeper, everyday, into depression." Can you relate to this statement? How? Explain.
3. Recall a time when someone who would usually tell you yes, finally told you the much needed no. How did you feel? Describe the outcome.

CHAPTER 11

First Steps Out

Dear Ed,

At first, I didn't think much of the meeting. While I never doubted the sincerity of the people I met there, they weren't like me. Most of them looked as if they never had a break in their whole life, and as if they hadn't shaved or showered in the last month. I wasn't like that, because after all, wasn't I "most likely to succeed"? Surely most of them weren't as sharp as I was; scoring well on entry tests for the military or attending a competitive school with submarines and sonar, like I did.

Then it struck me: no, they weren't like me. They weren't like me at all, but... *<u>I was like them</u>* .When I listened to each of those people–really listened to them–and when I listened to the people who were running the meeting, I finally saw what I had become. While laying in the Drop-inn Center I cried and cried, crying for the loss of the old Donald Whitehead. I felt sorry for myself because of that loss, and I hated that loss and where I allowed it to lead me. Until then I never faced myself. My mother came looking for her son's body, but I never looked for myself.

Then, I did.

Most Unlikely to Succeed

At the second meeting, I paid attention to what was being said, to all of the concepts and all of the words and what they meant, not only in general terms, but what they meant to me. I began to see, perhaps for the first time, that even though I was an addict, even though I cried myself to sleep on mats at the Drop-Inn, I was still someone who with high potential and great inner strength. I went to a third meeting, and then a fourth. At one of the meetings, I even got up to talk and to tell people about me. I was shocked by their reaction and what they thought of me. They seemed to value what I said; they seemed to think what I was saying was not merely about me but other people as well. Although I could hardly have known it, I had now taken my first steps on the road back. I was at the bottom, but I was looking up, not down.

It wasn't easy. Not at all. For one thing, I was continuing to live at the Drop-Inn and that was hard for me. In addition to the desperate homeless people who had nowhere else to stay, there was the staff. The staff consisted mostly of former addicts (if such a term can ever have any meaning), and of the formerly homeless; people who were two steps ahead of the rest of us. Some of them had their own problems, to say the least. I remember that some of the staff were always angry, always reaching out for some kind of confrontation. I remember some staffers who yelled at everyone, no matter what the need. Sadly, I remember some of the staff simply didn't care; and they gave up not only on the people living at the Drop, but on themselves as well.

Just as there were some bad staff members, there were some outstanding people among those in charge. Ed Deering was one of the kindest. Ed was over 6 feet tall and probably close to 250 pounds, with a rolling baritone voice that could shake a mountain (and shook me a few times). When I made the decision to genuinely seek help for my addiction, Ed was the Director of the treatment program. The treatment program–the Drop-Inn's live-in treatment community–was tough. Very tough. We went to a meeting every night, and we worked at the shelter during the day.

We spent our time serving meals to the residents, cleaning up, and volunteering in the community as if there wasn't enough work at Drop itself. In addition, on Saturday, we worked at Re-Stoc, the Drop's housing program in the deep poverty area of Cincinnati, Over-The-Rhine. Re-Stoc was an acronym for the Race Street Tenant Cooperative, a program that took over old, abandoned buildings and rehabbed them as affordable housing. The work at Re-Stoc was tough: gutting buildings and construction, yard work and painting and drywall–and anything else that needed to be done to rebuild a spot for someone in the community.

Most of the guys in the program hated the work at Re-Stoc, finding it physically demanding, and with little reward. But I enjoyed every minute of it, although for a strange reason. I got to talk to people. All of my life, I have been a talker and a listener, and it was at Re-Stoc where I first did some of my best listening, and then some talking of my own. And through talking, I met some people who would have an influence on my life. I met Andy Hutsell, a tireless advocate for the homeless (and still working in Cincinnati today). How many lives has Andy saved? And I met Amy Harpenau, a woman whose ideas and courage have meant a tremendous amount to me.

Also in the Drop-Inn program was a guy who would become one of my best friends ever, and truly an inspiration. His name was Jimmy Heath. Jimmy was a talented and intelligent man, and although we didn't hit it off at first, we grew to develop a mutual respect for each other while we shared life in the program at the Drop-Inn. Our relationship was cemented by a series of articles about us (and others) in the *Cincinnati Enquirer,* authored by Krista Ramsey. The interview we did with her for those articles helped us learn about ourselves, the lives we led prior to the Drop-Inn, and the roads that brought us to our meeting in this place so far from the beaten path.

I met buddy gray, who changed my life more than any other human being I have ever met. First of all, "buddy gray," is the correct spelling of his name; buddy always preferred that his name be in lower case, because that was always how he thought of himself. Buddy came from a middle-class background, but the way he lived his life he was the most upper-class person I ever met. Buddy founded the Drop-Inn Center in 1972, and both he and the Drop-Inn immediately became a cause and a lightning rod in Cincinnati. Buddy believed every human being was obligated to any other human beings in need. And buddy believed it was necessary not only that each of us should act individually, but also that we had an obligation to act collectively to right the wrongs done to the poor and the weak.

Buddy began what I think of as his ministry right at the end of the Vietnam war, and he was already seeing what heroin and other hard drugs (remember, cocaine was yet to emerge) could do to those who were too hard pressed to avoid them. Buddy started the Drop-Inn with only his own funds and a few companions but right away he began to make a difference in Cincinnati. And for this, he was loved by some and despised by some.

Buddy was a man who saw only the black and the white of things, and he was a ferocious fighter for the rights of the poor, and he took in hand any weapon he could find, any weapon he could meld to his need. One of buddy's most useful tools was an entity that most homeless persons would never have seen as a weapon at all: the homeless buildings in the poverty-ridden sections of Cincinnati. Buddy would stake a claim to these buildings with the theory being he would agree to rehab them and to put them back into the community as low-income housing. In no time at all, buddy became one of the largest landlords in Cincinnati. At the same time, buddy lacked the funds to do more than one building at a time. Soon some of the more powerful people in the area decided buddy was the problem instead of the solution. The man who was trying to do the most was being blamed because he could not do ten times what anyone else was doing.

I met buddy when I went over to the local Greater Cincinnati Coalition for the Homeless, an organization that buddy did not start but certainly one he rebuilt and revitalized. Buddy seemed to recognize in me some sort of talent and strength and he began to slowly coax out of me what I had done my best to destroy with alcohol and cocaine.

And buddy was tough. By the time I met him, he had already been at work–or at war–in Cincinnati for well over a decade, and so he knew what it would take to succeed. He held me to fierce standards, but he also gave me something to have of my own, the "something to live for" one always hears about. After about three months, buddy made me an outreach worker at the Coalition. My job was to go out onto the streets and to talk to the poor and the homeless, to try to get them to come to the coalition where they could have a safe place to live and decent food to eat. I found it a long, hard job. Not many people knew or cared about the Coalition, even after being informed..

But some did, and I kept after those few. I was starting to see in myself what a reason to live for and what belief in a cause could do. I was determined to help those people, and through that growing passion, I was very slowly starting to come up from the hole of alcohol and cocaine I had dug for myself. I worked as an outreach worker for over a year, and then buddy decided that it was time for me to move up. I became Outreach Coordinator, and for the first time, I was given some responsibility. I found an apartment in which to live, certainly nothing special in any way, but a place that I could at last call my own. It wasn't much, as they say, but it certainly beat the cold hard floor of the Drop-Inn.

I went back and attempted to mend the disaster I made of my family life. I talked to my mother and told her how I was doing, talked to the woman who came looking for my body, and I told her I was finding a purpose in life, and I was going to make it back from my personal hell. I remember how my mother cried.

I remember how I left her, after she and I cried and cried some more, and I returned to my new job as Outreach Coordinator for the Greater Cincinnati Coalition for the Homeless. In no time at all, I was doing even more. In fact, I was astonished to find myself so busy that I had actually stopped thinking so much about alcohol, drugs, and my addiction.

What I was thinking about was how to help others; I was learning to look at life to see tremendous injustices flourishing right under the eyes of each and every one of us. buddy started to take me to meetings on homelessness, and I met some of the people with power in Cincinnati: council members and commissioners, businessmen and bureaucrats, professors and agency heads. I went with buddy to meetings in Cleveland and Columbus and I saw the problem of homelessness was just as bad in other cities and municipalities. I went with him when we and some others helped to start a fledgling Coalition on Housing in Ohio. I was meeting people and seeing things, and above all, I was, for the very first time, beginning to sense that I, Donald Whitehead…Donald Whitehead, the addict …might be part not only of the problem, but of the solution.

Dear Ed,
Thank you for having a voice that shook mountains and even me.

Something to Talk About...

1. Describe a time you felt sorry for yourself. How did you turn the situation around?
2. Consider the steps in the 12-step program. Which step do you consider the most difficult and why?
3. Recall a situation which led to you wanting to help others.

Chapter 12

A Small Success and a Great Tragedy

Dear buddy,

But, as good a friend as he was to me, buddy gray had made some serious enemies. At the heart of buddy's problem lay real estate. In Cincinnati, as in any major urban community, the laws of real estate and the economics of real estate are two very different animals, and buddy was determined to have a hand in both sides of things.

buddy believed in low-income housing, an opportunity for people locked into poverty to find a place they could afford and keep. But while buddy was gaining control of more and more property in return for his promise to refurbish those properties, he rarely had the resources to begin work, and as a result, buddy soon found himself under fire from other landlords, especially the larger renters who had the most to lose when buildings technically scheduled for rebuilding lay dormant in bad condition while buddy sought funds. The problem, though, was buddy needed funds for more than a few projects; in addition to the shattered and broken buildings he now owned, he was also still in the process of building the Drop-Inn Center into a first-class shelter, and he also had a number of other irons in the real estate fire at that time. buddy believed he was taking formal control of abandoned properties and that he would eventually rebuild these properties. His critics believed he was only supplying homeless persons with abandoned buildings in which they could stay, and he never really planned to rebuild those properties at all.

I, of course, knew buddy meant to rebuild every property he acquired, but at the same time, I have to admit it was hard to see where the resources for all of those projects might come. The City of Cincinnati was reluctant to invest in low-income individuals. They had other plans for Over-the-Rhine required the displacement of many if not all of its current residents. I knew buddy was genuinely planning to re-do the properties, because buddy and I were spending more and more time together. During any week, we might be in Columbus for a housing meeting, back in Cincinnati for a battle with Cincinnati's city council, off to Dayton for more meetings, and all the way up the state in Cleveland.

As a result of those growing demands on his time, buddy had given up his position with the Coalition, and a young man named Pat Clifford became the Executive Director. Pat was a strong advocate for the rights of the poor in Cincinnati, but fairly quickly buddy realized that he needed someone with a college background and some serious managerial skills to assist him at the Drop-inn Center itself. buddy felt the Drop would be best served if he himself were not seen as its only voice; after all, buddy realized he was making enemies at a rapid pace–it was at about this time we started to see signs up in Over-the-Rhine with the phrase "no way, buddy gray!"

These signs referred to buddy's acquisition of yet more properties would have to wait for resources.

Pat Clifford agreed to become the Administrative Coordinator of the Drop-Inn at the same time he was

Executive Director of the Coalition. At that time, I saw myself as no more than one among a group of recovering addicts who seemed to be tagging after buddy while he took on battle after battle for the poor and the homeless. I hardly sensed anyone believed I possessed leadership potential, but buddy saw me differently, and he told me so. He told me I still had the ability that I then believed to have been forever gone from my life. He told me that I could be one of those few people who could make a difference. He told me I could someday even become the Executive Director of the Greater Cincinnati Coalition for the Homeless or some other program.

At first, of course, I wasn't convinced. But with buddy's help—and his badgering—I finally began to think that maybe I could come out of the hole I dug for myself, and maybe I could yet become the sort of person who could do things for others. Maybe there was a little spark left of most likely to succeed.

I experienced a hard time, but eventually I caught on as I started to take on some leadership myself. After all, buddy had taken me to enough meetings that I at least had some guidance as to what other people in other cities were doing to overcome their problems. And buddy himself remained as my guide. He helped me in a hundred ways every week.

Yes, buddy helped me right up until the day he was murdered.

buddy gray was shot and killed at his desk in the Drop-Inn Center by a man who lived in the same building he did, a man buddy had helped. The day before, buddy and I had attended a meeting, and I remember everything about that meeting. I remember coming back into Cincinnati with buddy, and having him drop me off at my apartment.

"Don't work too hard," he said. I remember that I smiled and then went inside. I remember that I made myself a few notes for what we were going to be doing that next day. The next day with buddy gray never came.

A former resident of the Drop-Inn, a man buddy helped, walked in and shot buddy. He said he believed buddy was ruining his soul and was attacking his spirit. And buddy gray, a man who had done more than anyone else in Cincinnati to help the poor and the homeless, to help the beaten and the downtrodden, was shot dead by one of those he helped.

When I heard the news, at first simply didn't believe it; there are rumors and stories that spread through any community. The homeless community is no different in that respect from a group of bankers hearing stories about the rise or fall of interest rates. Except this time, the story was true. My friend and my mentor was dead.

Dear buddy,
Thank you for your sacrifice.

Something to Talk About...

1. What is the state of low income housing in your city? Where can you get more information?
2. Recall a time when you agreed to take a job, position, or role you didn't initially think you could handle. Why did you feel this way? What happened next?
3. The author writes about a tragedy involving someone who was a key influence in his life. Describe a similar traumatic event in your life.

Chapter 13

More Steps Up and…an Emmy?

Dear Alphonso,

Buddy's death was a gut wrenching blow to me. Only a few days earlier, my other grandfather died, another shock, but it was nothing compared to what I felt when buddy died. I felt like a man who loses a compass in the woods; not only lost, but angry. I was angry at myself because I felt in some way I should have been able to stop what had happened. I was angry at the landlords because I felt–and I feel to this day–their opposition was a contributor to buddy's death. And above all, I was angry at fate, angry at God, and angry at life itself. How could buddy gray–my friend, my mentor, and in many ways, my savior–how could buddy gray be dead? Unfortunately, yes, buddy was dead.

Donald Whitehead was alive. No matter how disturbed I felt about that juxtaposition, it was a fact I was alive. Suddenly, it hit home for me the void in the cause of homelessness in Cincinnati. We held a first-rate funeral for buddy, with people from all over the country attending, and we mourned buddy for months. Even as we mourned buddy, the chasm in leadership lay over us like a heavy cloud.

In a few weeks, we sorted out things as much as we

could. I applied for the position as Executive Director of the Drop-Inn, and so did Pat Clifford. Pat was chosen, and I agreed with that choice: Pat had a college degree and had been the Administrator, so his selection as Director of Drop only made sense. What also made sense was Pat could only do one job, especially without buddy to guide us all. I then applied for the position as Executive Director of the Coalition for the Homeless. And to my surprise, I was chosen.

Now, I would like to say that I sat down at the Director's desk, and immediately began to make a difference in Cincinnati, but the truth is that I sat down and then asked myself, "okay, now what do I do?" Still, it was a fact I was Executive Director of the Greater Cincinnati Coalition for the Homeless, and another fact people looked to the Director for leadership. And to be truthful, I was more than the Executive Director in Cincinnati. Buddy had pushed and dragged me onto the board of COHHIO, the Coalition for the Homeless in Ohio, and he had seen to it that I started to become well known in even national homeless circles. In one instance, buddy talked me into going along with him to a national meeting in Dallas, a joint effort with the National Veterans Administration. Buddy told me I would be on a small panel; instead what he should have said was that I would be on the keynote panel for the entire event.

I started—slowly—to build on what buddy had built, to structure what buddy had tried to structure and what he had been structuring when he died. I took buddy's spot on the executive committee of the National Coalition for the Homeless in Washington D.C. I went onto the executive board of COHHIO, and back in Cincinnati, We started a new street newspaper called "Street Vibes" that would serve as a model for giving a voice to the homeless. I developed new funding sources for the Cincinnati Coalition, and I started a television interview show using the new cable access facilities.

I was determined to do as well as I could with what buddy had started and I was also determined to sort out my new thoughts and ideas. I wanted to use the experiences that shaped my thinking and to weld those experiences into the passion buddy showed and kindled in me. I also continued the work buddy started with the National Coalition for the Homeless, working with groups in D.C. on vital issues, and meeting the people who had their hands on the policies and procedures regarding funding the programs we needed. I met people in HUD and the Department of Health and Human Services, and bureaucrats from FEMA and the Department of Education. I met with senators and congressmen, and learned some of the political realities of the world, and I slowly–very slowly–learned what it meant to be involved at a national level. Running the Greater Cincinnati Coalition for the Homeless was quite different.

I remained Executive Director of the Greater Cincinnati Coalition for the Homeless from 1998 until 2000. By the end of that period, I felt certain the Coalition was on a firmer footing regarding its ability to function financially and we built strong relationships with the city infrastructure, including the Mayor and Cincinnati's City Council, as well as other power brokers citywide. Michelle Budzek stands out from the group. The city hired Michelle to develop an application to the Department of Housing and Urban Development (HUD) for a multi-million dollar grant as part of a planning process between entitlement communities and the nonprofit world. The partnership with Michelle soon became a "best practice" and helped bring over one hundred million dollars into Cincinnati to combat homelessness). Unfortunately, for every Michelle Budzek, there remained a host of others who neither understood the needs of the homeless nor even cared. Still, even in that environment, I admit I built stronger relationships with other groups in Cincinnati. I still blame some of the landlord groups for instigating such a hostile tone against buddy, and in that way contributing to the cause of buddy's death). And I'd started a new life on a social level as well, by becoming a parent, and it was that event that, in fact, started me on another aspect of my career.

While I cared, lived, and breathed for the cause of homelessness, the one point of all my work starting to haunt me was the paycheck. It wasn't just the size of the amounts I was earning; it was the uncertainty as to whether or not the paychecks would even appear. At an event called a "Standdown," I met some people from Goodwill Industries which was, at that time, running programs for homeless veterans under the Department of Labor's HVRP (Homeless Veterans' Reintegration Project). It didn't take me too long to see they were pretty good at what they did, but I also saw they knew strategies I didn't know, especially about grants and federal and state proposals. When they offered me a position as manager of their new Census program, I reasoned the Coalition was in good enough shape for someone else to take it on, and I owed it to my new family to find a better-paying job. Goodwill not only paid better, but it also kept me in the thick of things in the fight to help the poor and the homeless. In many ways, it was ideal.

At Goodwill, I made new friends, especially Charlie Blythe, the Grants Manager, and John Briggs, who did so many things. I stayed with Goodwill for almost two years, learning everything I could about federal grants and state proposals. I saw how my new colleagues found their grants and I learned how they managed the actual writing and positioning of their work. It was all new to me, and I turned out to be an apt and quick student.

At the same time, a surprising and wonderful opportunity happened in my life and it all came about because of my love of drama and the stage. I was hosting for an evening at the

"Go Bananas" Comedy Club in Cincinnati, a gig I started to do regularly, when another performer told me about a movie holding auditions at the Cincinnati Arts Consortium in the West End right there in Cincinnati. I thought about it for a while, and then my love of drama got the best of me; I knew my chances would be pretty slim but I felt I had to try. When I went to the audition, I was shocked: there were over six hundred people trying out for roles, and it turned out many with professional experience, something I lacked. I read over the roles for the characters posted, and finally one caught my interest: the lead character's stepfather, who was abusive and illiterate. The more I looked at the description of the character, the more I became intrigued, and by the time I got a chance to read, I felt I almost became that character, whose name was "Melvin." Possibly because I had to wait a very long time in a hot auditorium, I was a little angry when I went in to read, and somehow my determination captured what the director envisioned. "That's Melvin," I heard him say. In the following days, I had another call-back to read again, and then a third call-back, unfortunately, I couldn't make. Because I missed the previous opportunity, I thought it was hopeless, but to my great joy, I got the part.

The director for the movie was a man named Alphonso Wesson, and I was amazed by his skill and gift, and as we began shooting, how much he was able to get out of me. The glamorous Piper Davis played my wife and my son was played by a little guy named Clive, who turned out to be the real son of a friend of mine. My part was shot in three hard days and the whole movie was shot in three weeks, mostly in Cincinnati, but with an ending in Paris. By the time the film was edited, we had a final title: *Open the Sky*. It wasn't until the first screening in Cincinnati when I learned it was Alphonso's life story.

When I saw the initial screening, I was astonished by how good it was, and the great talent of the film team. I have to say I enjoyed every minute and I loved and was proud of what I accomplished. But when it was over, it was over. Or so I thought, a couple of months after the screening Alphonso called to say that he was going to submit the movie to the National Academy of Television Arts and Sciences. He told me he was also submitting several of the characters in the movie for individual awards and he thought my chances of winning were good. He called to ask my permission. I was stunned. I felt like I did a good job but this was beyond my wildest expectations. If I died the next day, I could go to my grave knowing I was nominated for a regional Emmy. A couple of weeks later I received word my nomination was accepted.

I quickly learned that I was competing against actors who starred in films in the seven Midwestern states, and so I was nervous to think of how important this really was. Being nominated for an Emmy was unbelievable. I was convinced there was no chance at all I would win but at least I got a free trip to the awards show as an "artist." In all _Open the Sky_ was nominated for nine Emmys (as I mentioned, it was a very good movie.) Most of the cast got together for the Regional Emmys at the Aronoff Theater in Cincinnati. We went to the Emmys with a great deal of fanfare, arriving in a stretch limousine in Tuxedos and evening gowns (even little Clive wore a tuxedo). I thought the Limo ride was the highlight of the evening but it turned out I was wrong.

Open the Sky received seven Emmys that night. Alphonso, Piper, Clive, and I all received Emmys for our performances. Clive is actually listed in the Guinness book of world records as the youngest person ever to receive an Emmy. It was wonderful beyond belief, and that night I really began to believe that all things are possible with God.

I still worked to help people in need, and handling the Census Program at Goodwill. But by its own nature, the Census program was never meant to be a long-term event, and so, when the Census project began to wind down, I turned my attention back to the cause of homelessness, (not that I had ever really left it). By the time, a situation had come up in Washington D. C. and could best be described as both interesting...and somewhat unpleasant.

The National Coalition for the Homeless has always been a tremendous tower of strength, not only in the bureaucracy of our nation's capital, but throughout the entire country, acting as a beacon to steer not only the programs of individual providers, but to guide the fight itself, to oversee what it actually meant to serve the homeless. For years, the Coalition fought for legislation, built alliances, and led the fight for a way to best serve the homeless. For years the coalition weathered storm after storm, and built positions and programs we all could use and lean on.

Then, in the year 2000, the National Coalition for the Homeless found itself in the middle of the perfect storm. To my shock, I was right there with them.

Dear Alphonso,
Thank you for trusting me with the role.

Something to Talk About...

1. Tell about a time when you needed to rebuild after being struck by personal tragedy or loss.
2. Think about this statement:"...there remained a host of others who neither understood the needs of the homeless nor even cared." What do you think the author meant by this statement?
3. "...I was shocked at how talented he was, and as we began shooting, how much he was able to get out of me." Describe a time when someone brought out the best or more than you even believed was in you.

Chapter 14

The National Coalition

Dear Bill,

The National Coalition for the Homeless (NCH) has always been a powerful champion of the homeless and poor. The coalition was founded on civil rights issues. NCH's founders believed in a right to housing and promoted housing as a human right. In many ways the plight of homeless people was the unfinished business of the Civil Rights Movement. Redlining and housing discrimination was disproportionally experienced by people of color. Homelessness among African Americans was more than a poverty issue. Regardless of color or ethnic background, people experiencing homelessness were under attack by law enforcement, business leaders, elected officials, and the general public. In 1999, the Coalition found those two targets–the civil rights of the homeless and the lack of affordable housing nationwide– to be in conflict. The Board of the Coalition–which had always been large and thus somewhat unwieldy–split in both numbers and power over which of those targets was the appropriate bulls-eye; the only thing people agreed on was that the two targets could never be a "joint venture," and resources did not exist for both needs.

Within a short time, the split grew ugly, with board members taking sides in anger, and the final result was a two-pronged wound: first, Mary Ann Gleason, the longtime Executive Director of the Coalition, was forced out of office when board members who strongly supported her and her position found they could no longer muster enough support, and secondly, when those board members–including some of the most powerful and respected names in the homeless community–resigned in dispute.

The agency was in a dysfunctional state. Uncertainty was palpable, it grew worse because our problems surfaced at the end of the Clinton Administration, a presidential administration reasonably friendly to understanding the needs of the homeless. In the brief time I spent on the national scene with buddy, I started to get a feel for what could be done, and I could see our potential opportunities were now in great danger. Even from Cincinnati and the viewpoint of Goodwill, it was clear the National Coalition desperately needed not only a way to mend the approaching breach, but even more immediately, a leader. What a leader we needed! The possibility of a hostile administration and a widening schism in our own ranks, seemed to increase the likelihood of finding someone with the leadership skills to keep the Coalition afloat and lead it to the safest ports. We needed someone whose credentials were beyond reproach regarding his or her understanding of homelessness, and whose approach would be acceptable to all viewpoints and whose skills could be used in the bureaucratic wrangling on "The Hill." We had no such person. Even from far away in Cincinnati, as a board member, I was involved in the hunt and saw the infighting permeating the process. I did my very best to keep an even keel and retain the respect of all sides. I felt I knew what we needed, but I felt equally as strongly that we would be unable to attract such a person:

too many potential candidates were too closely aligned with one side or the other of the schism, or in some cases, were even unwilling to move to Washington, D.C., an absolute requirement of the job.

Finally, however, both sides seemed to agree on a single candidate who, while lacking some of the supposed requirements for the position, still had the respect of all concerned and was thought to have the ability to succeed. I was surprised to find myself only peripherally involved in what seemed to be the final discussion, and it wasn't until I received a surprise phone call that I learned why.

I was the candidate! I, Donald Whitehead, who slept on the floor of the Drop-Inn Center and was snatched from misery by other people, was now thought to be worthy of such a trust.

I began by saying "no." I couldn't imagine myself learning to handle the power corridors of our nation's capital at such a crucial moment in the Coalition's history. Surely, I thought, there had to be someone else, there had to be someone who could do that job. They couldn't really want Donald Whitehead of Drop-Inn Center fame. I called Bill Faith, my friend—and buddy's good friend—in Columbus, Ohio. I asked him if he knew about the process. Bill said he did, he did, indeed. It turned out that Bill was one of the mainstays in advancing my name and candidacy. Bill and I began to talk. I argued that there simply HAD to be someone else. "Who?" Bill asked. I had been through the candidates and I had no real reply. I was too inexperienced, I argued; I lacked the skills; I was unknown to legislators. Bill replied that the position would not be unknown and that as Executive Director of the National Coalition for the Homeless, I would have some power on my own. I would learn to use it, he said.

I talked with other people. Those other people voiced

other arguments: there was no candidate with reasonable stature whose elevation would not destroy the Coalition, they claimed. I was well-liked and viewed as having the ability, if not the immediate experience, and my own homeless background was a huge, huge plus. I would be speaking with the voice of someone who actually knew what it was to be homeless. I would be speaking not only from the heart but from the gut. And so, it turned out I was chosen as the new Executive Director of the National Coalition for the Homeless. I, Donald Whitehead, was to run a national organization charged with defining a philosophy that could mean everything to every homeless person in America. Suddenly, all the struggles, disappointments, heartaches, and despair seemed to be a distant memory in the rear view mirror of my life's journey. My decision to try recovery in August 1995 was validated; when I went to the first Narcotics Anonymous meeting, they told me anything I dreamed I could achieve and all I had to do was stay clean and work hard. Now that declaration was coming true for me.

As I accepted the job as Executive Director of NCH, I was filled with hope. I knew I had the ability to change the perception of homeless people forever. I was the first formerly homeless person elected to a position at this level. In just 5 short years I shifted from abandoned buildings and restless nights on Fountain Square to an office on 14th Street near K Street in Washington D.C. Once I started on my recovery, I surpassed other peoples' expectations (even my own) every step of the way. There were proclamations from the City of Cincinnati, the media covering my going away party, with state and local politicians, and my family and friends attending. I didn't believe anything could be better. When I arrived in D.C., I sensed a surge of hope inside. What could have been better? What really could have been better?

Then, I walked into a perfect storm.

An interesting observation about the storm was how hard it was to recognize. During my first year as Executive Director, we raised more money than the organization ever brought in before, and we were staffed at the highest level the organization ever saw. For the first time, the National Coalition for the Homeless (NCH) had the resources and the staff to effectively carry out its mission. In short, all seemed at least somewhat well.

Enter the storm.

Twice each year, we met in a strategic planning session—the board and the Executive staff—and for my first meeting. I anticipated a honeymoon period during which the arguments that split the board could be set aside. I was wrong. The old problems did not away—as I hoped—but intensified instead. Half of the board lead by Sheila Crowley and Bill Faith—the man who had recommended me for the job—wanted to focus again on affordable housing production and scale back our work on civil rights, the same conflict of ideas from before. The other half, led by Lynn Lewis from New York and Paul Boden from San Francisco, still wanted us to focus on protecting the rights of people experiencing homeless. It was not only a source of division at NCH but a split in the homeless movement itself, an ideological divide that would change the face of the homeless movement. This second episode of an emerging paradigm shift would alter the face of homeless programs across the nation. At NCH, the split caused an exodus of board members that would damage the organization for years to come and even to this day limits its ability to be relevant in the chaotic world of Washington D.C. I was horrified by what happened. This split, along with the emergence of an administration with a

Most Unlikely to Succeed

new attitude of punishing the homeless for being homeless–was phase one of the perfect storm.

Phase two was a much smaller impact, but still one that hampered anything I might have wanted as Executive Director. After the forced departure of Mary Ann Gleason, the NCH staff became one of the first national advocacy agencies to unionize. The union–an incredible ally to those in hostile work environments–was not nearly as useful in work situations where hostility was not present. Although we were staffed at record levels, the truth was we were still a very small agency, and the small size of NCH's staff made the union burdensome on management. For instance, I found my time was to be taken up with what I considered to be small, internal matters with no weight in the battle against the great foe of homelessness; I found myself dealing again and again with events I considered trivial, events about someone's idea of how to gather little bits of power versus significant mission focused ideas and opportunities. I found myself bogged down with the minutiae of employment paperwork and the residue of every small problem magnified over and over.

The final element of the perfect storm was, of course, the newly elected Bush administration. I expected things would be different under a Republican President, but still I held some hope and belief in the new President's stated view of "Compassionate Conservatism." However, I quickly learned "Compassionate Conservatism" was merely the new brand name for "Trickle-down Economics," this view of money and resources has hatched so many of the problems in modern homelessness. For me, Trickle-down Economics is very much like rain on a roof: some may indeed trickle down onto the roses underneath your (eaves?) but the majority by far is caught by the gutters and shunted into a sewer system. I soon learned, most members of the new administration believed otherwise, even with mounting evidence of renewed homelessness staring them in the face. It became a common event for me to speak with someone who held a radically different view and with no intention of listening to what we had to say. I felt again and again as if they wanted to school us. I often wondered how many days these men and women spent in the Drop-Inn Center, or if they had ever seen a homeless shelter.

Looking back, I suppose a more experienced director could have weathered this storm and brought his organization through unscathed but that's not who I was. I was Donald Whitehead, the new guy learning on the job. Every day for me was a new experience with new problems and a fractured and unwieldy board of fifty-seven people, all with differing views of what should and could be done. But still, I thought we could and would make it. And then, just as I thought we were about to turn the corner, my life turned upside down with a single phone call from back home in Cincinnati. Just when I was starting to feel confident in my position, just when I was starting to have success, my whole world fell apart.

Dear Bill,
Thank you for believing I could do the job.

Something to Talk About...

1. What do you know about The National Coalition for the Homeless?
2. Describe an experience in life where you wore many hats and juggled many responsibilities.
3. Recall a time for you, "Just when I was starting to feel confidence, just when I was starting to have success, my whole world fell apart."

Chapter 15

Tragedy: No Other Word

Dear Kadeash,

I was in a meeting at the National Coalition headquarters when I received the dreadful phone call from Cincinnati. My daughter was in the hospital, and she was not doing as well as people hoped.

If there was anything in any way positive during the horrible years of my addiction–anything at all–it was I fathered two children. My two children–Kadeash and Cortez–were the loves of my life. Neither one of them were planned; both were, in fact, the result of random gratifications of passion. Circumstances could have deemed my babies as "throw-away" children. To me they were everything good and I loved both of them dearly. Among my deepest and greatest regrets is missing out on all of the early and formative years of my daughter's life. Kadeash's mother–a family friend who I dated–was too afraid during my addiction to tell me I had a daughter. What a daughter she was! Kadeash was the perfect child; a little angel about whom no one had anything bad to say. She was a straight-A student who loved to sing and dance, and she loved her family. Kadeash was a preemie, but there was nothing premature about her achievements. As a doting parent, I must say she was an astonishing little girl, a wonderful child, and a great daughter.

She was also ill, very ill.

I can honestly say, after "I cleaned up my act" and got into recovery, I tried to be the best possible parent to Kadeash and Cortez. At that point in time, thanks to my Executive Director's salary, I had the resources to provide needs and wants for my children. I lived in a home in the eastern portion of the greater Cincinnati area, and I flew back from D.C. to see my children as often as I could. When I was in town, the three of us were as close as could be, and I wanted to give my children all of the things that I had never had as a child. The most precious gift from me to my children was the attention of their father.

Kadeash was sick.

I caught a quick flight out of D.C., and I remember nothing more about that plane ride other than it seemed to take forever. A few weeks earlier, Kadeash went to the school nurse because she had a stomach ache, but I assumed it was nothing more than the usual problems of childhood. Now I was being told that my daughter was in the hospital and it was not because of "usual problems."

When the plane landed, I got a message from Kadeash's mother that struck me like a tidal wave: my daughter was not just in the hospital; she was in intensive care. I drove directly from the airport to the hospital, and I was horrified at Kadeash's condition. There was no doubt at all that she was clearly ill. For the next few days, her mother, my family, and I lived at the hospital with me calling back to my office in D.C. only to keep the lightest contact. I stayed in touch with Kadeash's mother (although there was never any possibility that we would get together) and helped to do as much for Kadeash as possible, and so it was hard for

Most Unlikely to Succeed

either of us to believe what was happening. And then, on the third day, we were hit by yet another tidal wave, but this time it was far heavier and more dangerous: they diagnosed my daughter's condition. The doctors told me Kadeash had leukemia.

Leukemia! How could that be? It was possible that the daughter of some other person in some other city, in some other state might have leukemia, but certainly not Kadeash, certainly not my daughter. Yes, she did have leukemia. On the fourth day, they began to treat her with chemotherapy. But my daughter seemed not to respond. During the night, she began to struggle even harder, she began to have trouble breathing and taking in oxygen. I stayed at her bedside every hour, desperately willing my little angel to breathe, to recover, and to give herself life. The doctors tried everything they could think of, and I prayed the whole time. But, as I sat there, helpless, Kadeash's condition slowly but surely worsened. The physicians tried strategy after strategy, drug after drug, and treatment after treatment; but by the early hours of light, it became apparent nothing was working, not drugs, not therapy, not chemicals, and not even prayer.

By dawn, my daughter was on life support, breathing only with the help of machines. It was around eight a.m. when the doctors seemed to almost give up as a group, and it was only a couple of hours later when they came in and counseled me. The doctors wanted me to give up, to take my daughter off the life-support machines that were keeping her alive. They told me the reality was she was gone, and there was completely and absolutely no hope. But I wasn't about to deny God the chance to pull off a miracle, and so I said no, there wasn't any way I was at all ready to make that decision.

By ten in the morning, I was instructed to call in

all family members; the physicians believed my little angel had reached the end of her short and beautiful life. Kadeash's mother had left the hospital for only a few short hours to try to get some rest, but then she quickly returned. As each family member arrived, I sat by my daughter's bed and tried somehow to comfort her even though I knew she could not hear me and that the daughter I knew was already gone. All we could do was watch as life slipped away from Kadeash. It was the worst moment of my life, worse than any instant of my addiction, worse than any moment of treatment. We sat there—all of us—and watched her oxygen levels slowly decline, and we watched her heart beat slower and then slow even more, and then we watched as the oxygen levels reached zero and her heart beat moved to a totally straight line. My daughter, my innocent angel, had died. I remember collapsing in a heap and for the first time in my life questioning my faith. I cried like a baby as friends and family held me up. I thought about how such pain could ever be so unbearable, how such powerlessness could ever be that numbing. I lost something that day: a piece of my soul died with Kadeash.

The next few days, I held myself together by making funeral arrangements. Somehow, my mouth would work and words would come out, even though those words had no real meaning. My family was amazing. They stayed with me for every moment, never leaving me alone for a second. My twelve-step family was there, too. They knew it was times like this when staying clean could still be the greatest challenge; they knew how easy it would have been to slip over and try to dull the incredible pain with drugs. My brothers, David and Darrin, my friends, and my sponsors Greg and Glen were extremely supportive. Looking back, I have to say they were the people who kept me going. Those were the men and women who saved my life.

My daughter's funeral was attended by members of my board, family, friends, twelve-step members, and many, many children, as well as friends from the community. It was incredibly sad, and my son, Cortez, took it so hard he was not able to stay through the ceremony. They say losing a child is unlike any other loss. They say it is so unusual there isn't a name for it. They have a name for the grief, a name for the pain if you lose your wife, husband, or parent, but not when you lose your child. Losing your child is not supposed to happen. Any parent foresees a living to an old age with a rich filled with honor and respect: the death of a child–that's just not supposed to happen.

I stayed in Cincinnati for three weeks and then flew back to D.C. where I buried myself in my work. I attended more AA meetings and more church services, and worked out at the gym more. bury myself at place after place and moment after moment, but nothing helped to ease the pain. I would advise anyone who has to face such a loss to seek counseling immediately because I can say to that person that the pain will overwhelm you and consume you and may even kill you. The pain is like open heart surgery every day, and even when it heals, the scar still screams every time you touch it. There is nothing like it.

I went through the next two years with daily struggles of grief and what I now realize was untreated depression. My work suffered, my relationships suffered, my life was turned upside down. It was the worst time of my life, worse than addiction, worse than awakening in my own vomit on the floor of the drop-inn center.

Horrible, horrible, horrible. I wondered if my life would ever get better?

*Dear Kadeash,
I thank God for blessing me to be your Daddy.*

Something to Talk About …

1. Describe a time when you experienced grief. What were some of the ways you coped?
2. The author wrote…"what I now realize was untreated depression." What do you know about untreated depression? Where can you find more information?

Chapter 16

A Different Kind of Recovery

Dear Donnie,

In the months after my daughter's death, I vegetated mentally and almost worked myself to death. I was putting in eighty hours a week, traveling all over the country, and trying to remind myself of how far I have come. I also reminded myself how far I could fall if I ever allowed my actions to go in the wrong direction. In the past three years, I lost my mentor, buddy gray, my father, my second grandfather, and now, my daughter. I was sad in a way I never imagined I could be, sad, shaken and maybe even broken. I was afraid; afraid of my own possible pending death. I reasoned, if everyone around me could die, then why would I not follow them? Was I somehow charmed? Somehow safe?

I was so depressed I hated going back to my apartment. Every moment centered on my position as Director of the Coalition, broken up only by the hours I put in at the local gym, and the 1 hour a day I spent at my 12 step meeting. I started working with a new sponsor named Alvin. Alvin lost a child as well, he could empathize with me in a way most others could not. I was slamming away at anything physical in an effort to stay on top of the rolling log that had become my life. I worked out two hours every night, and I worked at the Coalition the rest of the time. I suppose I ate and slept but I don't remember. My mind and my body worked; my heart and my soul sank into a vegetative state. I dated but those dates were mere shells of what any relationship could ever become. I would look into another person's eyes and imagine the pain of losing yet someone else in my life. I was so depressed and so lonely, and yet, at the same time, I was terrified of getting close to anyone. The thought of death remained my close companion. Even in the midst of my emotional turmoil, the Coalition and I still made accomplishments. Working with other groups (in Washington, very few individual agencies accomplish much on their own), we made great strides in collaborative efforts with the National Affordable Housing Trust Fund, an effort led by the Coalition for the Homeless and the National Low-income Housing Coalition, and strongly supported by groups across the country. We dedicated a full-time staff person to that early effort and collected thousands of endorsements to help the campaign become a bill that finally passed in 2008. We worked with advocacy groups to pass legislation to improve access to schools for children experiencing homelessness.

For education policy, we hired Barbara Duffield who became, and continues to be, one of the country's leading advocates on the education of homeless children and youth. This again was a collective effort with NCH at the center. Only those in this movement know the true significance of providing access to education for homeless children. Also, the drafting and introduction of the Bringing America Home campaign may yet prove to be a paradigm-changing moment years from now. This campaign was the most comprehensive piece of legislation to address homelessness in American history. It contained provisions allowing HUD to reshape the delivery of homeless services, especially in areas such as allowing the definition of homelessness to include people surviving in hotels and living in other doubled-up situations.

We spent a lot of time challenging the then-new Chronic Homeless Initiative. The Chronic Homeless Initiative was based on studies produced by Dr. Dennis Culhane of The University of Pennsylvania. In his studies, Dr. Culhane found that 10% of the homeless population consumed 50% of the resources. As a result of this, the Chronic Homeless Initiative proposed to use a very large amount of all federal resources on this population, which was defined as being "single homeless persons with a disabling condition who were homeless for a year or more or who had had four episodes of homeless in three years." The theory was that if you removed these chronically homeless individuals from the system, it would release resources for the other 90% of the population whose homelessness was more episodic. The policy that followed was a combination of Permanent Supportive Housing or Housing First under which the chronically homeless would be taken from the streets and placed directly into housing.

The problem with the policy is that while it can be (under certain circumstances) effective for the population it serves, it leaves the majority of the remaining homeless population without adequate resources. Families with children and single adults without a disability are left with limited housing options. In our white paper "Poverty versus Pathology," we identified the results of this policy and its impact on family homelessness. Unfortunately most of what we predicted has materialized and family homelessness has exploded with HUD now being forced to add chronically homeless families to the eligible population for these scarce resources. At NCH, we fought for a comprehensive approach to address the diverse needs of the population and went beyond the emergency measures of chronic homelessness.

During my time at NCH, I met many important people. I of course met President Bill Clinton and then-Senator Hillary Rodham Clinton as well as Secretaries of HUD Andrew Cuomo and Mel Martinez, and Tommie Thompson, the Secretary of HHS. I met and came to know many senators, including Senator Reed, Senator Kennedy, Senator Harry Reid, Senator Dodd, Senator Voinovich, and Senator Mike DeWine. I dealt with so many Representatives that it is difficult to note all, but I will mention the ones for whom I developed respect and visited with many times: Representatives Julia Carson, John Conyers, Barney Frank, Dennis Kucinich, Barney Sanders, Jan Schakowsky, Jesse Jackson II, Steve Chabot, Howard Dean, Barbara Lee, Steney Hoyer, Stephanie Tubbs, John Corzine, and Carolyn Kilpatrick. There were also civil rights leaders such as Coretta Scott King, Martin Luther King III, Al Sharpton, Dick Gregory, Jessie Jackson, Dorothy Height, John Lewis, and Kim Gandy.

I was interviewed by all major television networks and cable networks including ABC, CBS, NBC, CNN, MSNBC, FOX News, and NPR. I've been interviewed by Tavis Smiley, Bill Cunningham, and Sean Hannity, and I've debated many conservative and liberal radio hosts, including Pat Robertson, Michael Medved, Sean Hannity, Bill Cunningham, and others. I've met and talked with entertainment celebrities Jerry Springer, Monique, Cedric the Entertainer, Steve Harvey, Bernie Mack, D.L Hugley, Isaac Hayes, Kathleen Turner, Dougie Fresh, and Wesley Snipes; and sports legends Magic Johnson, Brigg Owens, Shawn Springs, and Joe Frazier. Through the State Department, we were able to provide homeless policy guidance to the governments of Brazil and Japan, and I was invited as a guest speaker at a fundraising Dinner for Jack Layton, housing advocate, and candidate for Prime Minister of Canada. I provided written and oral testimony before the 107th, 108th, and 109th Congresses, and I received two awards of Special Congressional Recognition as well as a leadership Award from the National Head start Association.

I helped raise awareness of homelessness by speaking all over the country at some of the most prestigious universities including Penn, Yale, Georgetown, American, George Washington, Howard, Illinois, Cincinnati, Maryland, Johns Hopkins, Iowa, North Carolina, Morehouse, Clark University, Loyola of Maryland, and Xavier. I delivered keynotes or addressed workshops at homeless conferences in Arkansas, Ohio, Minnesota, Colorado, California, Oregon, New Mexico, South Carolina, North Carolina, Washington State, Iowa, Nevada, Florida, Vermont, Kentucky, Indiana, Maryland, Arizona, Tennessee, Puerto Rico, Massachusetts, Michigan, Delaware, Pennsylvania, Texas, Washington, Virginia, Georgia, Montreal, Canada, and finally in Toronto, Canada,

When I arrived in Washington, my hope was to build a movement. I studied the early Civil Rights effort and worked on building alliances with the current Civil Rights movement and student groups. We did, for example, successfully organize actions in places like Covington, Kentucky where we convened a march in response to civil rights violations against homeless people, and our action drew individuals from states as far away as Maine and resembled some of the early actions in the Civil Rights Movement.

Finally, looking back on my years at NCH, I would have to say funding challenges prevented my dreams from materializing but I have not abandoned the idea of a homeless movement. I'm satisfied with the tremendous effort I and others put in while at NCH, and I only wish I could say I was completely satisfied with the results. Still, I did my best; I did my very best.

Dear Donnie,
Thank you for traveling the road to recovery.

Something to Talk About...

1. The author calls this chapter "A Different Kind of Recovery". Recall a time when you were on a personal road of recovery. How did you get there? Where did you go from there?
2. Describe a time when you were going through "emotional turmoil" and were still able to make some accomplishments.

Chapter 17

Tracy

Dear Tracy,

Even with all my accomplishments, I still couldn't shake the pain of my daughter's death, and the fear of my own mortality. Hopelessness lingered. Then a friend said he knew someone I "really" should meet. At first, I wanted nothing to do with anyone I "really" should meet, but my friend was persistent. So persistent, in fact, I finally agreed to meet this mystery woman. To my great surprise, meeting her was different. In fact, it was far more than different; it was wonderful. My love life was unfolding like a chapter in a romance novel. Her name was Tracy. She and I exchanged phone numbers. We immediately started talking long hours on the phone. I came back to life. Somehow, the heart crushing burden of my daughter's death and how it followed the other losses in my life, began to ebb. The heartache came closer and closer to bearable.

Tracy had two children, two daughters: Channing and Devin, who were the pride and joy of her life. At first, I found even the mention of her daughters to be painful because they were only a few years past the age of my own dear Kadeash. Tracy's warm, intelligent, understanding, and kind response to my loss was just what the doctor ordered. In fact, after a few dates, I guess I earned enough points in Tracy's estimation to be granted the chance to actually meet her daughters. When I did, I saw just what my Kadeash would have become, Tracy's daughters were little angels. The kids were standoffish at first, but after a little while, the girls seemed to like me and to give me the thumbs up. And soon enough, Tracy and I became a couple, seemingly destined for each other. Throughout my life, I have believed God places people in each other's path for a specific reason, and I have to believe I saw the hand of God setting Tracy in my path.

Tracy and I learned from each other in many ways. Tracy's parenting skills were amazing. She devoted herself to her girls in a way I'd never seen before and it paid off for everyone. Channing was a straight "A" student and one of the most beautiful and kindest spirits I have ever met. Devin was younger and more mischievous but just as kind and talented. Tracy maneuvered both girls like a maestro conducting a symphony she knew well. Tracy was a magician of a parent and I loved watching and learning from her. I had plenty to learn. I'm patting myself on the back believing Tracy learned some things from me, especially how a gentleman acts in a relationship. I pride myself on being a gentleman in any term of the word.

When Tracy and I moved in together, Channing decided to go live with her dad. So it was Tracy, Devin, and me. Tracy and I built a solid relationship, even during our tough times. Communication and honesty kept our relationship together. I have never trusted a person as much and I have never shared my feelings so openly. We also worked on our relationship quite a bit. We read relationship books like *Woman are from Venus and Men are from Mars* which were quite helpful in strengthening our level of communication.

We learned about working on our relationship while on our first vacation together. We traveled with two of the nicest and wisest people I have ever met: Gordon Packard and his wife Elizabeth. Gordon invited us down to his condo in San Carlos, Mexico. San Carlos was a lovely town across from Baja, California. There is nothing quite like the ocean for a young love, especially in a regular town away from all the tourists with their cameras, and each morning and evening Tracy and I would watch the sun rise and set over the gulf. In the evenings, we enjoyed insightful conversations with Gordon and Elizabeth. They shared the secrets to long loving relationships.

We spent a week in San Carlos and experienced the real Mexico, not Cancun or Tijuana but the authentic Mexico with all its fascinating and rich culture. That trip was the most romantic time I have ever spent, and it was easily my best experience with love. Toward the end of our trip, Gordon and Elizabeth presented us with a book by Diane Rheem called *Toward Commitment*. By the time we returned, both Tracy and I had read the book, and in the following months, we read it over and over again, as we reflected on our time in Mexico. As time passed, we would go on many more trips and we had a great relationship but there was no re-creating that week in San Carlos.

Tracy and I stayed together for four years, during which time I left the National Coalition for the Homeless. Regarding the Coalition, I would like to think that I left it better, but I have to question if that was the case. My departure from the Coalition was not graceful; in fact, I did something I had not done in a very long time: I resigned, I quit. By the end of my tenure, the organization was facing bankruptcy, and large numbers of staffers had left. Things imploded. Even with our legislative achievements, I have to question if anyone facing that perfect storm could have managed anything other than merely keeping the ship afloat. In the face of a hostile administration and a divided board we persevered and we weathered some successes against a perfect storm.

Today, however, although I continue to be active on the Coalition's Speakers Bureau, some members of the Coalition board have re-written history, forgetting the circumstances and the collective failure of the organization as a whole. Many have placed the blame for the very difficult period squarely on my shoulders. This is an easy and common practice in Washington, one President Obama faced and other Presidents faced the same revisionist sniping. The Coalition, at that time, had a deep, fundamental problem brought on by the sharp disagreement between members of the board. The fund-raising challenges we faced were not only the fault of the Executive Director but also the fault of something much deeper in the Coalition itself.

Since I left the Coalition, I have raised tens of millions of dollars as a private consultant, a grant writer, and a development coordinator (by the way, I still hate fundraising), and so I am very confident of my abilities in that area. Washington D.C. is an elite and unforgiving place which attracts the best and the brightest. Many, if not all, of these people come from a background of well-known universities and have a string of letters after their name. In this environment, a flawed person, a man who slept on the floor of a homeless shelter, is unlikely to be accepted without a degree from that well-known university or those letters after his name. In my world, overcoming barriers like addiction and poverty are things to be celebrated; but in the capital of the richest country in the world, the existence of those circumstances is to be feared and avoided. The idea the fight against homelessness should be led by someone who once *was* homeless seemed to some people a worthy thought, but in our nation's capital, that idea was an anchor so heavy no ship could ever sail with it. Over and over again, I've spoken with bankers, businessmen, and foundation officers, and I have presented our ideas with a passion and a sense of deep commitment; but when I have shared my own personal history, I quickly learned I was making a mistake: I learned the greatest point of pride in my life was viewed as a weakness.

Later on, in my consulting work, I learned to leave out my personal history and, as a result, there have been times when I walked out of an office with a check. Today, when I give a speech, I begin to talk while dressed as I did when I was on the streets. But underneath the tattered clothing, I always wear a coat and tie, and so, as I begin, I am face with angered and fearful listeners, but as I progress, I slowly shed the battered rags and reveal that I am indeed wearing that suit and tie. In no time at all, I hear the beginnings and then the roar of applause; but in Washington, it was always the suit they were applauding, and to them a formerly homeless man was always "least likely to succeed."

Tracy and I split in late 2006, our relationship was burdened by the weight of raising two teenage stepchildren (my son joined us) who didn't get along. We were both devoted parents whose commitment to our children outweighed even our commitment to each other. We loved each other deeply but at that point in time there were too many problems to overcome. It was not our moment there and then. We parted amicably, no fussing or fighting or bad scenes: we made a conscious decision to move on, and move on we did. I wondered if I would ever have anything again as rich as the days and months I experienced with Tracy.

In early fall of 2007, my son and I left the east coast and Washington D.C., and returned to Cincinnati. In need of work, I called my friend, Charlie Blythe, at Goodwill. By this time, Goodwill had built one of the most complete programs for homeless persons that I had ever seen. Goodwill in Cincinnati had continued as one of the Department of Labor's premier HVRP (Homeless Veterans Reintegration Project) grantees, and then had developed six other programs for housing and training. I took over and began to run a permanent housing program for the disabled, and at the same time as I worked for Goodwill, I rejoined the board of Cincinnati's Continuum of Care and also rejoined the board of the Drop-Inn Center. I have to admit, each time that I go to the Drop-Inn, I can only half-shiver in remembering how I got there the very first time and how I lay on a mat in the back of the building, on the cold floor, and cried and cried. What a long, long trip it has been.

I quickly returned to the business of helping homeless people. In some ways, I found it certainly less challenging than the work I had done on the "Hill" in D.C., but in a lot more ways I found it somehow more "honest" and much clearer in both effect and purpose. Each and every one of these clients needed what I could give them (and more), and they had no bureaucracy to push, no views to foist on me. There was a desperate need to somehow get back some little bit of their lives, some chance to have what I had. One thing surprised me: none of them in any way ever took me for one of them. A few friends and my family from the old days knew what I had once been, but to these people I was someone powerful, someone who could help them.

As I listened to each story, I became more and more engrossed in the everyday misery of these souls, and I slowly forgot the storm I barely survived in Washington, D.C. I ran the permanent housing for the disabled program through all of the remainder of 2007, and then through 2008. I had good friends at Goodwill and finally started the memoir you are now reading. It was a time when I had an opportunity to stop and to think not only about homelessness but about who I had become and what I wanted in the remainder of my life. It was a time in which I was finding a restful peace, but also a time in which I felt less challenged. I began a college program in Theology, and tried to develop a formal idea system regarding homelessness. It was a time in which I watched the politics of our country change, and it was a time in which I changed.

Then Tracy called.

Dear Tracy,
Thank you for loving me.

Something to Talk About...

1. What is one of your most memorable life changing relationships?
2. The author wrote, "Each and every one of these clients needed what I could give them ..." Can you relate to this statement. Explain.

Chapter 18

At the End...the Start

Dear Cortez,

Although we hadn't seen each other since our decision to separate, Tracy and I hadn't lost contact; we spoke at least twice a month and shared our triumphs and disappointments, the ups and downs of our children's lives. I remember once when we spoke, Tracy was going into the hospital for minor surgery. I talked to her just before she went in, and I talked to her again just after she was released, but the next several times I called, I was unable to reach her. In fact, she had returned to the hospital for a twenty-two day stay, although I am happy to say, she was then released a second time in much better health. The idea of Tracy being hospitalized was frightening for me.

At that point, although things were going well professionally at Goodwill and with Cincinnati's Continuum of Care, my personal life was hit with another emotional upheaval. I was disappointed in his behavior and it would have been an understatement to say that he and I were not getting along well.

Soon enough, Cortez requested that I allow him to move in with his mother, which I had no choice but to allow because I was never granted full custody. I reluctantly allowed Cortez to move out, heartbroken that he was willing to give up on all the progress he made in the last nine years, and frightened at the thought of what might happen next. A number of my friends always wondered why I never moved forward with gaining full custody prior to that time, but, although I never gave them an explanation, my reasoning was simple. In my heart of hearts, I was never sure about Cortez's paternity although I had been by his side from the day he was born and I had been the best father I could have been. The simple truth was I wasn't sure what a paternity test would reveal. Still, under the threat of having Cortez return to life with his mother, I knew I had little choice; I felt that in order to save him from a life of hardship, I had to remove the threat of his returning to his mother anytime the going got tough, and the only way I could do that was to establish full parental custody.

It was almost like losing Kadeash again. I was on the verge of a state of depression. I went to a meeting and shared what had happened with my sponsor. Everything seemed to be falling in on me. I felt as if I might be going mad.

Finally though, it came to me I was holding a pity party for myself with only one invited guest. After a couple of days' thinking, I realized this DNA test was just a test and it really didn't change anything. No matter what the results disclosed; it didn't erase my feelings for Cortez.

Maybe he wasn't my biological son but he was still my son in every other way. It was hard to always keep those thoughts in mind even though I gave it my best shot. I was still hurt and I needed some relief.

Tracy called, and I told her what had happened. Although we'd talked many times over the past two years, this seemed different. As we talked and she shared her thoughts and ideas with me, it became clear we were both interested in seeing each other again. She called a second time and then again, and soon we were regulars on the phone. Our conversations over the next few weeks were different, more substantive; and we spent a great deal of time reminiscing about our relationship until it finally became clear that this was something we both really missed. Moreover, neither of us was in a committed relationship at the time.

As fate would have it, I was planning on traveling to Washington to speak at an event for *Live It, Inc.* A Waldorf-based organization I helped to start, and so Tracy and I decided to see each other while I was in D.C. We started by going to one of our favorite casual dining spots, Red Lobster, for a dinner. We spent hours together and soon it was if we had never left each other. When I finished my speaking engagement, I had to leave, which saddened me greatly, but over the next few months we decided to see each other as often as possible. Getting to know each other again was amazing. We both made several trips to Pittsburgh–the agreed upon mid-point–by car, and we each made several flights, Tracy to Cincinnati and I to DC. It was during one of the last trips to Pittsburgh we made the decision to get married. It was not really a shock to most people who knew us and were close to us. In fact, as we quickly learned, they always assumed this day would come. We set the wedding for October 25, 2008.

Over the next few months we not only planned our wedding but tackled a major decision as well: where would we live–Cincinnati, Silver Spring, Washington, D.C., or somewhere else? This was an extremely tough decision. Tracy had her daughters, Channing and Devin, to think about. Channing was a senior at the University of Maryland scheduled to graduate in June with a degree in education, and Devin was in college working on her own degree in psychology. I had my family as well. Cortez was now living with his mother, in an undisciplined environment that was anything but what I wanted for him, but I was still very much present in his life and felt I desperately needed to be so. There was my own mother whom I love dearly and whom I had absolutely adored being close to over the past two years. In Cincinnati, I also had my brothers and sisters whom I was able to see regularly for the first time in about five years.

On Tracy's side, she also had her mother, and dad, and brother. The biggest question was the employment, and that swung matters more toward the east coast area of Baltimore and Washington, D.C. because Tracy had an outstanding job in the Baltimore area, but little knowledge of Cincinnati. So, in the end, we felt that there was no choice except for me to move to Tracy's area (especially since I was already fairly familiar with the geography due to my time as head of the National Coalition). We settled on Laurel, Maryland, a small town in Ann Arundel County halfway between Washington D.C. and Baltimore. All I can say about my own family is that my mother and my siblings understood the need for us to locate as we did.

Before the wedding, we moved to Laurel, Maryland, where we quickly found a place that seemed appropriate to both of us. Even though I was commuting back and forth between Maryland and Cincinnati, I immediately started looking for work in the homeless arena, and I'm happy to say that I was able to land a job on the first interview I had, with St. Vincent de Paul of Baltimore (SDVP), exactly the kind of agency I have advocated on behalf of over the last 20 years. SDVP had fifteen programs addressing homelessness comprehensively in the Baltimore area, working on chronic homelessness, substance abuse, family homelessness, prison re-entry, and education. I worked at Beans and Bread, a program in downtown Baltimore that housed four sub-programs: a soup kitchen that feeds 400 people a day; an outreach center that provides referral and outreach services, medical services, and access to substance abuse treatment; a transitional housing program for 20 men; and a scattered site program, for 60 chronically homeless individuals. My role as Assistant Director was a dream role: I could manage housing for homeless people and have direct contact without the administrative and fundraising responsibilities I do not enjoy.

On October 25th Tracy and I hosted our beautiful, small, private wedding in Cincinnati. October 25th was one of the happiest days of my life. I was getting married with all the people who I loved by my side. The wedding party consisted of Channing and Devin and my brothers Darrin and David. Cortez, and Tracy's nephew, Niles, were the ushers. My favorite cousin "Ink," was there, and two of my best friends, David Mizell and Joel Davis, sang a song at the reception, written by Tracy's brother, Tony. Our Mothers sat proudly at the front of the church. Everything went perfectly that day, and we even found out Channing was expecting. What an amazing beginning to our new lives.

We spent the next week in South Carolina on our honeymoon, enjoying our new happiness; we locked out the rest of the world and started planning for our future together. I arrived in Laurel for good in early December. I really enjoyed my life at this moment; this was all I had ever really wanted: a loving wife, a decent job, and a family. Channing moved in with us a week later, and it felt really good to have both girls under our roof. I got along well with both Devin and Channing, who is the most beautiful spirit that anyone would ever want to meet. She was close to graduation but still working full time, and she cooked for us quite a bit in the first couple of months that she lived with us.

Most Unlikely to Succeed

My life had come full circle and I felt I was finally at peace. One of the difficulties of life as a recovering addict is the constant need for more, for better, for bigger, never ever being satisfied. But I was satisfied with my life in Laurel. Tracy and I had a "date" night every Friday because we were committed to keeping our marriage fresh, something we had learned in pre-marriage counseling. I thrived during my dinner table political debates with Tracy and Channing, where I was usually double teamed but the debates were refreshing.

We were in an incredible time, the start of the age of Obama, the age of the audacity of hope. Our family was completely immersed in this new hopeful America led by the first African American president. Just like most African Americans and frankly, most of America, we followed every story and every news clip leading up to the most important inauguration of our time. On a personal level I was so relieved after advocating in Washington during the Bush Administration when the policies of that administration almost made me lose faith in my country.

Tracy and I decided we would both try to attend as much of the inauguration as possible. In January of 2009, Washington was electric. The entire downtown was slowly filling in anticipation of the Obama inauguration. We spent weeks planning our personal experience with destiny, and we could hardly wait. We decided against going to the mall on the day of the inauguration because of the long lines, the terrible cold, and the transportation nightmares. Our plan was to spend a day celebrating Dr. Martin Luther King Jr.'s birthday and then head down to the mall the night before just to be there and to feel the electricity. It was an amazing day. We watched the original footage of the civil rights movement at a theater in Silver Spring, one of only two places in the entire country where it was being shown. I don't care how many times I see the footage; I am always moved beyond belief by the incredible courage and perseverance of the people in the movement. The entire audience was in complete silence throughout the viewing and in concert we all let out a huge round of applause at its completion. The footage made you angry and then encouraged you, and then made you angry again, and it finally ended with encouragement beyond belief.

After the showing at the Silver Spring Theatre, we headed downtown. When we arrived, the electricity was apparent immediately. The downtown D.C area was filled with all things Obama; tee-shirts, posters, hats, buttons, umbrellas, and everything else you could imagine. There were thousands of people and a diverse mix of humanity. People were singing and dancing and talking like never before. There was an air of love. It was kind of a modern day Woodstock without the drugs, sex, and rock and roll. The media outlets were amazing and they underscored the magnitude of the event. We spent hours on the mall watching the live filming of the Chris Matthews show and seeing media vans from city after city. The electricity in the air that day made my whole journey real in the magic of that evening.

The audacity of hope—the theme of the election—could be the theme for my life. Against all odds I answered Langston Hughes's question from the poem Harlem, "What happens to a dream deferred?" For me, the answer is… nothing happens to dreams deferred; deferred dreams are still there waiting in the recesses of our mind, waiting like a flower or an unborn child, waiting for the chance to be released. And just like a flower or a newborn child, deferred dreams just need a helping hand to bring them out. And now I have a helping hand (and have had helping hands from so many people in the past), and thanks to those helping hands, I now hope—and believe—that my dreams will no longer be deferred.

Dear Cortez,
Thank you for being my son. I am proud of you.

Something to Talk About…

1. Have you ever felt betrayed? Explain.
2. Describe your "dream deferred" and "audacity of hope".

Epilogue

My life has always been a rollercoaster ride. This fact did not change and life did not run smoothly even after returning to the area and marrying Tracy. One terrible crash still lay in wait. How many times have I experienced the joy of accomplishment or discovery only to quickly encounter pain?

The day after the inauguration, a day filled with promise and hope, we experienced a tragedy beyond belief. We were both sitting at our computers watching and reading different inauguration stories when we heard the doorbell. We were surprised because we never got visitors. At almost the same moment, the phone rang and it was Mark–Channing's biological father--and he was speaking, but I couldn't quite make out what he was saying. I could tell, however, that he was in a lot of pain. I answered the door and it was two highway patrolmen. My first thought was that it had been another escape from a nearby youth detention center, but it was anything but. The patrolman asked for Tracy by name and I thought she must have had an outstanding ticket or something; the last thing on my mind was an accident. Horribly, I was wrong. The patrolman sat us both down and told us the horrifying news that Channing-Tracy's wonderful daughter-had been killed in an accident.

We were both floored. Surely someone had made a mistake. But it was not a mistake. Channing had been killed when a tire had come off of a vehicle being towed down I-495. The dislodged tire had rolled across the highway, hit an 18 wheeler, flew up in the air, and landed on top of Channing's vehicle: she never had a chance. Both Channing and Reagan (her unborn child) had been lost to us.

The pain for my family was devastating, and for me, it opened up the wounds I felt when I lost Kadeash. In many ways, Channing had become so dear to me because I had imagined that she was the kind of person that Kadeash would have been had Kadeash lived. Channing was such a kind, gentle person with such a warm heart. She was a 'straight A' college student who was already starting her career as a teacher. She often talked about spending her own money to buy things for her students who came from underprivileged backgrounds. With her and Tracy, the last few months had been among the best of my life. I was thoroughly enjoying my new marriage and our new family life. The rollercoaster turned over on me again.

I worked very hard to provide Tracy all the support she needed as she made arrangements. She was extremely brave although her heart was ripped to shreds. My understanding of God is one I've often imagined while flying above the clouds. The beauty of the clouds is unsurpassed but as we dropped lower I started to see civilization and I realized this is how God sees us. He can look down and see ahead for miles. He can see a bridge miles ahead of us. Sometimes he steers us clear of the place where there is no bridge and at other times he works another way, sending people into your life who have already found a safe way to avoid a fall in the missing bridge's direction. In some ways, I believe God sent me to Tracy because he knew I'd experienced the missing bridge and maybe I could help her make it to the other side. I did that in those horrible times following Channing's death, and I will continue to do so in the future.

Looking back over what we have written, I realize some readers will not understand the underlying theme of this book. In the beginning, I wrote that I wanted to inspire people; I wanted to help people in hard spots to see that they could put their abilities to work and step away from those spots. I've been told that my story is unique and that it might not be one that can be duplicated, because of some considerable talents that I have. I thank those who have shared that comment. But if there is a theme to this book, it is that I truly believe we all have unique talents and skills that can assist us in overcoming the barriers that trap us in the quicksand of poverty, homelessness, and addiction. I have heard it said that we should not let our situations become our destinies, and I would like that to be the message of what you have read. If you are struggling today, look inside yourself to find the gift or talent you can use to lift you from your current situation. Find it and grab it; find it and hold on to it. Believe me, it's there; it's there for all of us and there for each of us, and it has the power and the strength to rescue us all. God Bless each of you.